D0788460

WHO'S HOLDING THE UMBRELLA

WILLIAM E. YEAGER

Thomas Nelson Publishers
Nashville • Camden • New York

Published in Nashville, Tennessee, by Thomas Nelson, Inc. and distributed in Canada by Lawson Falle, Ltd., Cambridge, Ontario.

Printed in the United States of America.

Scripture quotations are from THE NEW KING JAMES VERSION. Copyright © 1979, 1980, 1982, Thomas Nelson, Inc., Publishers.

Library of Congress Cataloging in Publication Data

Yaeger, William E., 1925-
  Who's holding the umbrella?

    1. Christian leadership.   2. Yaeger, William E.,
I. Title.
BV652.1.Y34   1984   253   84-22694
ISBN 0-8407-5430-2

To my wife, Barbara,
and our children:
Linda
Robin
Mark

Contents

ACKNOWLEDGMENTS
PREFACE
1. Learning Lessons the Hard Way 11
2. The Umbrella Man 23
3. Setting Up the Umbrella 38
4. The Nature of Spiritual Leadership 54
5. Selecting Your Leadership 71
6. The Care of Other Umbrella Men 89
7. Courage to Confront 102
8. Four Crucial Steps in Leading by Example .. 121
9. Stand by Your Man 138
10. The Umbrella Man as Decision Maker 153
11. The Accountability Group 170
12. The Reward Is Worth the Struggle 186
    Epilogue: Two Little Words 202

Acknowledgments

I want to thank the people and the pastoral staff of the First Baptist Church of Modesto, California. Together, they have proved the principles of leadership this book describes.

I am particularly grateful to Maxine K. Lewis, who worked tirelessly on the manuscript.

I also wish to express my grateful appreciation to Lee Roddy for his editorial assistance.

William E. Yaeger

Preface

This book was written in the hope that other Christian leaders will be helped and encouraged. It was long in coming. It was written partly in response to the needs expressed by pastors and lay leaders who have shared their hearts with me during their participation in the Institute of Church Imperatives. Many of the problems these men and women have brought to light are dealt with here.

It is worthy to note that of the countless problems and hurts these Christian leaders have singled out over the last thirteen years, spiritual warfare and intimidation by other church members are consistently high on the list. Thus, I have written from my own experiences as a pastor in the hope of giving encouragement to others with these same concerns.

I have attempted to keep the book on a positive note, but there are subjects discussed here, gritty issues, which cannot be left out of a book that deals with spiritual leadership in today's world. As you read, I pray you will look for those things that will help you to build the Church of Jesus Christ so that our Lord may exert His mighty power through His people.

I have found great joy and satisfaction in being a minister of Jesus Christ and a pastor of one of His churches. I hope you will hear that joy coming through. May the Church of Jesus Christ rise up with one voice, as a mighty army in these days of tremendous opportunity—that we can make His light shine in the darkness.

Learning Lessons
the Hard Way

My first three lessons in leadership came in rapid succession and with much drama. The first occurred in January, 1945, near the close of World War II. The event was the invasion of the island of Luzon in the Philippines. Everyone in the squadron was excited; at last our forces were returning to Manila where General Wainwright had held out so valiantly against the Japanese invasion in 1941–42.

Our TBF Avenger, a torpedo bomber, had just caught a hook and lurched to a stop on the deck of the small ship, called a jeep carrier, because it was only 450 feet long. As soon as the pilot taxied forward to park, the three of us piled out of the plane to clear the deck for our fighters. This was all very exciting for a crew whose pilot was twenty-two; the turret gunner twenty-one; and me, a radioman and stinger gunner, nineteen.

I moved into the catwalk along the edge of the flight deck to watch the rest of our planes come in. Operating as a composite squadron, we had both Wildcat fighters and the Avengers. Our skipper, Captain Mack, was our squadron commander. His combat air patrol had just cleared the air of suicide planes that were operating from bases all around us in the islands.

Captain Mack was right behind us in a Wildcat. I could see him clearly as he made his approach. The skipper was a real leader, taking our squadron through the Surigao Strait to Lingayen Gulf and the invasion of the main island of the Philippines. Flying from the deck of the U.S.S. Kitkun Bay, our mission was to protect fifty troop ships and then support the troops when they landed. We were to act as flying artillery for them in their advance to Manila.

After a near-perfect approach, Captain Mack's plane touched down. To our horror, his plane's hook missed all eight cables. He slammed into the wire barrier that was thrown up like a fence to stop him. The Wildcat flipped over, leaving the captain hanging upside down from the open cockpit.

I jumped from the catwalk onto the deck as the crew rushed to help the skipper. He was unhurt, but a crewman, trying to help, reached into the cockpit and released Captain Mack's safety harness. I grimaced as he fell out, smashing his head against the oak-planked deck. I was afraid his skull was injured, but he got up, spat blood, and went below.

Lesson One: The Leader Leads at Any Cost

The flight surgeon grounded Captain Mack, but the next morning before daybreak he was back on deck anyway. We were within range of twenty-seven enemy airfields, and every available fighter in our squadron was needed to defend the task force. It was getting daylight when I again stood in the catwalk alongside the flight deck. I was in my third year in the Navy. I had started in dive bombers and would serve on three carriers in less than a year.

In the first light of dawn, the skipper's aircraft flashed by me as he led the flight off. Suddenly, I saw Captain Mack's head slump forward. The little Wildcat veered off the deck and plunged sickeningly toward the ocean. We lost him in the water.

His death was a terrible blow to us all. I wept that day, sad to lose our skipper, but I knew I had seen the passing of a tremendous leader. I had learned the key principle that made him great: a leader leads, no matter what the cost.

Lesson Two: Lead or Others Will

The day after the skipper died, a Japanese suicide plane struck us amidships. We abandoned ship in the waters off Manila. The squadron was miraculously intact and was transferred to another carrier in time for the battle of Okinawa, barely three hundred miles off the Japanese mainland. Waves of kamikaze suicide planes from nearby Japan attacked us. From the island of Formosa to the south, we were attacked by even greater numbers. We were to have seventy-three consecutive days of combat.

There I received my second lesson in leadership: where no leadership exists, other leaders—good or bad—will arise. A leadership vacuum *never* remains.

This time I stood in the pilots' ready room where all air crews were assembled for a briefing on what was expected to be a tough mission. When we were all present in our flight gear, we were told we would fly a major strike against a heavily defended enemy airfield on Formosa. We had to destroy the suicide planes on the ground before they could sink our ships at Okinawa. The mission required that two carriers sail partway south and launch aircraft to fly the remaining distance to the target.

The squadron commander who had replaced Captain Mack was an officer who liked to be called "Joe," the kind of man who wanted to be "one of the boys." But Joe was no leader. The briefing was nearly over and the mission fully outlined, but Joe had said nothing to encourage the men. That is when the second lesson in leadership began to take effect.

One pilot called from the back of the room. "Let's just drop our bombs in the water and get out of there!" Somebody else echoed the idea, "Yeah! Let's just hit and run!"

I could not believe what I was hearing! Even though I was a teen-aged enlisted man, it was evident to me that some of our team of officers wanted to take the easy way out. My eyes went to the new skipper, expecting him to rebuke the faltering pilots and give us a pep talk.

But Joe was not mumbling a word. He just sat there. He was supposed to be in charge, but he would not take command. Captain Mack would have said, "Listen, boys, this is going to be rough. But you follow me, and I'll take you there and bring you back."

Finally, another bomber pilot stood up in the back of the room. "I didn't come here to drop my bombs in the water!" he snapped. "Let's do what we came to do!"

It was amazing to see how that man's few words affected the briefing. The mood changed at once. The other pilots began to agree, their voices popping up all over the ready room as one: "Yeah! Let's go get 'em! Let's do the job we came out here to do!"

The pilot in the back became our leader. He directed us to our mission and challenged us to do our best. He inspired us with his dedication. We flew that mission without a single loss, although the other carrier lost two Avengers.

It was more than another combat mission for me. From that time on I would reflect often on the sharp contrast in leadership of those two commanders. One led the way, even at the cost of his life. The other man had the title, but he would not lead. Oh, he flew the lead plane and set the course to the target, but leadership is not merely performing technical functions publicly. Leadership is guiding others, motivating and inspiring them when they are afraid to do (or do not want to do) what they *must* do.

I have never forgotten those two lessons, now some forty years later: the leader goes first, regardless of the cost; and when no leadership exists, others will arise and someone will take over. Just owning the title of leader does not make a leader. But there's a third principle.

Lesson Three: The Leader Genuinely Cares

My third lesson in leadership occurred after the war when I was home on leave in Tucson. My parents asked about my experiences. I told them of the Kitkun Bay and how Captain Mack had been lost. They were predictably sorry about his death, but what amazed me was that they spoke as though they had known him.

I asked, "How did you know about him?" They told me they had once come by train from Arizona to visit me at my California base, but they could not get in to see me because I was in the base hospital with a highly contagious strep throat. As they stood outside in discouragement, Captain Mack came the long distance out to the main gate to speak with them. He assured my folks I was all right and was doing my job for the country. I was not sure he actually knew who I was at the time. When they explained about Captain Mack's personal kindness to them I was again deeply moved. And that was my third lesson in leadership: the leader genuinely cares!

Leadership Needs Procedure

After returning to civilian life, two other important events gave me further insight into effective leadership.

A year after my navy discharge, I was working for a public utility company in Los Angeles when a power failure blacked out a section of the city. A short had developed in an underground power cable, causing circuit breakers in the power station to kick out and shut down transformers in an underground vault. My job required me to work those vaults. Although I was not working on the day of this particular event, I knew the men involved.

Ralph Jacobson and his helper, Ben Wilson, were sent as trouble-shooters. After some minor repairs, Ralph cleared the circuit. But when it was energized, it kicked out the breakers in the power station again. Then a terrible thing happened.

The station operator held the circuit breaker handle down; the safety precaution provided by the circuit breaker was no longer there. High voltage exploded at the point of the short and the ground in the vault where Ralph and Ben were working. A ball of fire filled the underground cavern, a space about half the size of a racquetball court. Ralph, a mass of flames, struggled through the fire and up the ladder to the street. Although Ben was also badly burned, he helped smother the flames engulfing Ralph. Three days later Ralph died.

An investigation showed the station operator had been given no established procedure to follow. He had held the handle down, thinking to clear the circuit. His act cost a man's life.

When leadership fails, somebody always pays the bill. Those entrusted with executive responsibilities in any walk of life must anticipate the worst and provide the directive for the people in their care. This includes the church, for there are times when it seems no one is in charge.

What About the Church?

I had little experience with Christianity until after my wife, Barbara, and I had our second child. In 1951, our son Timothy suddenly became violently ill on his twelfth day of life. He died that night in the Children's Hospital in Hollywood.

In our time of crisis, people from a little Baptist church nearby reached out to us in loving concern. They stood by us; they prayed with us, and they showed us the way to the Savior. As a result of the shattering experience of losing a child, Barbara and I came to Christ and began our new walk with him.

The first church business meeting we attended, however, almost ended our regeneration before it started. Talk about a baptism of fire! It was the best argument I have ever seen for strong church leadership, for the first Wednesday of the month was "fight night" at the Baptist church. At first, I thought I was in a union meeting, except there was no smoking and cursing—just endless yelling and hassling. Barbara and I looked at each other

17

in wonder. Was this the way the church was supposed to be?

The Christian people who had prayed with us and hugged us after the death of our son now were engaged in political outrage and debate. Was Christianity all this anger and salvation, too? I had seen better behavior at the PTA.

After the meeting, Barbara and I did not talk much. For a long time that night I lay awake, wondering why it had to be so. Where was the pastoral leadership I had expected—and sorely needed—in my own newfound faith? Then, in the wee hours of the morning, I remembered my second lesson of leadership: where no true leadership exists, other leaders will arise to take charge. That night, almost everyone had moved into the leadership vacuum—I believe they call that anarchy!

A Call to Ministry and Church Leadership

After our first year as Christian believers, God called me to the ministry. Our new pastor, Fred Fels, gave me opportunity to serve and helped us interpret our call. In preparation Barbara worked while I went to college and then pastored a church during seminary days. My natural interest in finding an effective leadership strategy was so strong I began a quest that has occupied my thoughts for these many years. My heart's concern was—and is—for the development of leadership in the church, both lay and professional. As I searched the Bible for specific leadership principles, God searched my heart for the right motives.

Why was I so eager to learn? My previous training and experience was not as a leader, but as a follower. I could not point to one command experience I had had in the navy. In fact, it seemed I had taken orders from just about everybody in life. My school and young adulthood experiences were basically consistent. I was not in charge of anybody or anything.

But when I became a Christian, I believe God began to give me insights into leadership for the ministry. Heaven knows I needed all the help I could get! In so doing, He brought back into my mind all of the experiences in which I had learned what careful leadership was all about.

The Word of God, especially on the subject of leadership, came alive. I searched out the biographies of the biblical patriarchs and apostles to see what they did—and why. Most of all, I looked to the example of our Lord Jesus Christ. He is the supreme model, of course, for all spiritual leaders. He was truly "the servant of all."

The Umbrella Man

My thesis is simple. There are quiet qualities of leadership that burn like fire in the soul. One does not need to be flamboyant, charismatic, or even outgoing to provide effective leadership. Quiet qualities are God-given and form the basis for one's responses in leadership situations. They become the convictions that launch action and direct a leader from within. These qualities are established by the Holy Spirit through the Word of God and by the example of other leaders.

"Umbrella man" is a term I use for the leader who gives himself to the ministry of Christ in such a way that he equips believers and provides abundant opportunities for them to serve. His ministry is spread out like a canopy or protective umbrella, under which others can grow and flourish—and eventually become leaders themselves.

At times, Christian leadership might appear to follow the same basic principles that work anywhere. To an extent this is true. Why? Because all sound and valid principles of effective leadership have common origins in God. All truth is God's truth. Therefore, while the leadership principles I speak of are essentially spiritual in nature, they most likely would not be seen that way by the natural man, or by one whose motivation is to be self-serving.

The man who seeks to serve himself has another set of convictions to follow. It includes self-aggrandizement, expediency, and vainglory. He ought to think more about the impossibility of trying to serve God and mammon simultaneously.

Demas attempted to serve God with the apostle Paul, but he marched to the beat of a different drummer. For a while, he coasted along. But in the crunch, Demas deserted Paul and returned to the world he loved. Demas's guiding principles were not godly, but worldly. As 2 Timothy 4:10 explains it, "Demas has forsaken me, having loved this present world."

For the umbrella man, quiet qualities of leadership are articles of faith. They produce the convictions that help him do what he should do, what he must do. The man who is firmly convinced in his soul that leaders lead—no matter the cost—will always step out and set the example. He will lead in good times and bad, when it is easy and when it is tough, because in him burns a conviction that gives him courage to act—even at risk. When the crunch comes and the pressure is on, this man is predictable: he still will serve God. When the smoke of battle clears, he still will be at the head of the column.

Some quiet qualities are within us because we bear the image of God; we seem to know them intuitively. Other principles are learned by reading the Word of God and being instructed by the Lord. By experience, these biblical principles are applied to our lives. And experience, by the way, *is* necessary for strong leadership. The best way—really, the only way—to learn leadership is to follow first, and thus learn by example.

Leadership by Followship

It is a fact that one must learn to follow before one can learn to lead. We only have to look at the example of the disciples: they learned to lead by following their Lord for three years. Learning by following can help us develop principles of leadership, the quiet qualities that guide intuitively, predictably. There is no need, after all, to invent the wheel over and over again. We learn best by following others who have developed God's quiet qualities of leadership. "As iron sharpens iron, so a man sharpens the countenance of his friend" (Prov. 27:17).

People may use various styles of leadership, but if they operate from biblical principles and from spiritual convictions implanted by the Holy Spirit, the results will honor God and bless the church. These principles are used daily by good leaders who recognize wisdom and know what works, even if they do not know where the wisdom comes from.

The balance of this book is an honest attempt to pass on these principles of leadership I have learned and developed over the years, along with numerous practical suggestions for keeping things well-oiled. I hope these insights will make a difference in your church and your life, as they have in my own life and at the First Baptist Church of Modesto, California.

I also will be using some illustrations from military history in this book. Do not be offended by that. The Old Testament is filled with accounts of battles and the combat strategies of God's leaders. In the New Testament we see the faith of a certain centurian who understood military authority and, through it, Christ's authority. If fact, Jesus said of him, "Assuredly, I say to you, I have not found such great faith, not even in Israel!" (Matt. 8:10).

Paul spoke of spiritual warfare and of spiritual armor when he said, "Put on the whole armor of God, that you may be able to stand against the wiles of the devil" (Eph. 6:11). In John's vision in Revelation, our Lord's return is pictured as a military conquest. "And the armies in heaven, clothed in fine linen, white and clean, followed Him on white horses" (Rev. 19:14).

So I will borrow from my maritime past not because I am a militarist, but because I believe it is time for the Church of Jesus Christ to start acting like the mighty, spiritual army it is intended to be. It is, after all, kingdom versus kingdom. And that is what this book is all about!

The Umbrella Man

An umbrella man is someone who spreads his umbrella to help others keep dry and comfortable in a storm. His umbrella offers safety and protection. It keeps his group together, maintaining the unity of the Spirit in the bond of peace, so no one is disoriented by the wind and rain. Spreading his umbrella is his way of serving the people he is most concerned about.

Mr. Smith ran the School for Promising Children. He wanted them to be able to do their best in everything. Some of the children were quick-witted, and some were slow. Some showed more promise than others. Regardless of their ability, Mr. Smith was sure his task in life was to bring out the promise of each child.

The Big Umbrella

Then one day he gathered the boys and girls for an outing. The weather looked threatening so Mr. Smith chose the large, heavy umbrella with the metal handle and spines rather than the smaller, wooden-handled one. He always thought about protecting his children. They roamed the fields for a while. Little Jacob began to cough, and Mr. Smith noticed the sky was turning black. Albert felt a raindrop, then another, and another.

Soon it was very wet out, with whipping wind and loud cracks of thunder not far off. Mr. Smith gathered his class very close and commanded them to stay under the big umbrella. Being rather frightened, they did.

Lightning flashes and pelting rain had them a bit unsettled, but Mr. Smith led them on. He was getting quite wet, but somehow he managed to keep his little charges under the big umbrella by holding it as far out in front of him as he could. Almost back to the main road, at the top of a grassy hill, Mr. Smith counted his promising children to make sure everyone was there. Suddenly a violent whiteness lit the sky all around them, and the sound that accompanied it was thunder—crashing, vibrating thunder. The children's shrieks could not even be heard above it.

Silence. No more wind. Then only light rain was felt on the faces as they looked around for Mr. Smith. He was on the ground, his fist stiffly welded to the metal umbrella.

Mr. Smith's umbrella had saved the class from the School for Promising Children, as Mr. Smith had known in the back of his mind that it might. "When I grow up," said little Jacob, who was still coughing, "I will be like Mr. Smith, wise and brave. I shall carry the umbrella for those who need it, and I shall remember kind Mr. Smith whose umbrella became a lightning rod."

The Servant as Umbrella Man

Like Mr. Smith, the spiritual leader must be an umbrella man. Unfortunately, he is also the lightning rod! His task is to establish a spiritual umbrella over the church so God's people may grow and serve.

The canopy of the umbrella is intended to be a spiritual shield. Its upper side combats error and drives away unbelief; its underside provides a wholesome, friendly, spiritual environment for the church where believers can worship and feed and go out again into the world to be salt and light.

As the spiritual environment is established, smaller umbrellas can be placed under the big one. Ministries for adults, youth, and children can grow. Work with singles, seniors, and people with special needs can blossom. Every one of them is important, but each ministry enjoys the shelter of the bigger umbrella.

The size and effectiveness of the church will depend on how big an umbrella the umbrella man can spread. Biblically, this will connect both with the sovereign power of God and the spiritual giftedness of the pastor. In the parable of the sower we are told that some produce thirtyfold, some sixtyfold, and some a hundredfold (see Matt. 13:3–9; Mark 4:13–20; Luke 8:11–15). While it is true that different church situations have different potentials for growth and expansion, it is also true that the capacity of leaders will vary. I want to establish the point that the church's effectiveness will depend greatly on the pastor. In every other undertaking in life this is true: the leader's capacity and ability to lead will establish the extent of an organization's success. Conversely, his failure as a leader will almost certainly cause his organization to fail or do poorly. Look at how leaders are valued in war, business, sports, and politics and see that in all of these endeavors they are vital to success or failure.

Some will surely argue that what is true in war or business is not true in the church. "The ministry is different," they will say. This is true in part; spiritual leaders are not to dominate people and overpower them as leaders often do in the business world. Peter said the same thing when he wrote, ". . . nor as being lords over those entrusted to you, but being examples to the flock" (1 Pet. 5:3). Knowing this, we are still left with the fact that the church's growth and effectiveness depends to a great extent upon the pastor and his capacity and willingness to lead.

Some others might complain that depending so much on the pastor is really expecting too much of man and not enough of God. To this charge a question must be asked. Why is it, then, that some churches grow and others do not? Is not God equally available to all? The truth is that God the Father is present in His fullness through the Lord Jesus Christ and in the Holy Spirit. He wants men and women who are called by Him to give themselves completely and unreservedly to Him and to His work. God needs *more* of man.

The umbrella man idea is a philosophy of ministry that sees the spiritual leader as a servant, shepherd, protector, equipper, and a provider of opportunities for service. Pastors, we are vital to the cause. Most of us view ourselves far too passively.

The Umbrella Man as Servant

As a servant, the umbrella man utilizes his spiritual gifts as his contribution to the church. He leads because that is his ministry. We have only to look at the biblical words that describe such leaders to see what the nature of leadership should be. The word for "leader" is found in Romans 12:8 and other places where we are instructed in the distribution of spiritual gifts. In this case, the one who leads is to do so with "diligence." The word in the original text means "first to stand." It means that leaders lead by going first. In its biblical usage it has the ideas of leading and caring. The pastor is first among equals. This kind of leader lays his life on the line for God's people to prepare them to serve God.

Sadly, however, there are those who think service means doing everything alone. A frequent complaint heard around churches goes like this: "Our pastor was a real servant to us for many years, but now he is gone and none of us is trained to do anything. He did everything from cranking out the bulletins on Saturday to preaching on Sunday. And he took care of all of the church business. What he didn't do, his wife did. She ran the Sunday school, played the organ, managed the church office, and led the women's work. Now they are gone and we need help."

The service the umbrella man performs is not like that. On the contrary, his work is to equip and train others for service and then let them serve. He has to multiply himself by leading others. That is his service.

Another word in the Bible that describes spiritual leadership is found in 1 Corinthians 12:28. It is the word "administrations." This is the word that was used by the Greeks to describe a helmsman, the one who steers a ship. This word and the word for leader seem to be similar. On the one hand, the leader *sets the course*, defines the objectives, and inspires others to join him, while on the other hand, the administrator organizes things and people and *steers the course* set by the captain.

I was once on a ship that was caught in the tail end of a typhoon in the Pacific Ocean. None of us had thought too much about who was steering until we hit rough water. The waves towered high above our ship and came pounding down on the deck with terrifying force and horrendous noise. In the storm, we knew we needed a good man at the helm, someone who could keep us headed into the waves.

The person who can guide the church through difficult times, always being careful to stay in the will of God, is like that helmsman. He is servant of all. That is what the umbrella man is, but he must first of all be a preacher and teacher of the Word of God.

A Solid Preaching Foundation

If you look around the country, you will see that in virtually every place where the church is healthy, meeting needs, growing in numbers, and reaching out in its world mission, there is a strong preacher in the pulpit. Spiritual gifts used in leadership may vary, but wherever the church is doing well, there is invariably strong pulpit leadership.

I say this because those who use their teaching gifts are very strong leaders, although they do not always think of themselves that way. They lead through their marvelous ability to teach the Bible. Their influence in leadership is clearly evident when the programs of their churches are given over almost completely to the teaching ministry. These men follow their gifts and lead accordingly. They are, by my definition, umbrella men.

What seems strange is that most pastors are reluctant to admit their roles in actually taking hold of the reins and leading the way. This is in part because many seminaries have taught a nondirective approach to leadership. The cry of "dictator" has been shouted so often in recent years that many men who are called to lead are ridiculed into passivity by peer pressure. I have even heard seminary professors scoff at "those strutting pastors," as though there were an unholy rivalry going on between teachers and preachers.

Of course, there are pastors who seem to think the numbers game is everything. Likewise, there may be some leaders who *are* dictatorial. But do not throw the baby out with the bath water! Leadership is a gift from God to the church and is a responsibility to be carried out by those so gifted. (Remember, too, that statistics are biblical. Someone was certainly counting heads in the Book of Acts!)

True spiritual leaders are not dictatorial. They seem to have the God-given ability to inspire others to want to do more for their Lord. They ignite people to action. This is done through the ministry of the Word of God and by their own examples. The apostle Paul was like that. He was not embarrassed to claim to be following Christ and he did not back away from saying, "For though you might have ten thousand instructors in Christ, yet you do not have many fathers; for in Christ Jesus I have begotten you through the gospel. Therefore I urge you, imitate me" (1 Cor. 4:15–16).

It is high time for God's people to look upon spiritual leadership as a blessing, not a curse. A group of pastors visited us some years ago. When they had been with us at the church for several days, one of them, who had been viewing our work with a jaundiced eye, said, "Look, how can you run an operation like this and be the servant of all?" The questioner had assumed that there must be something wrong with leadership when the program flies and God's people get things done— and have fun in the process. Like many, he made the word "servant" synonymous with "doormat."

To answer to his question (which was really a statement) I at first found myself on the defensive. It was as though I had done something horribly wrong. Then I replied, "Leadership is a responsibility and a service. The pastor must know that he is an under-shepherd serving the Great Shepherd, the Lord Jesus Christ." Then, for the first time, I drew a rough picture of an umbrella on the blackboard and tried to explain how the umbrella man is a servant of all. Anyone who thinks that setting up a spiritual umbrella is not a service to the church has never had much real leadership experience.

Once on a camping trip, I had to set up the center pole of a tent in a howling gale. By the time the tent was up and my family members were all inside warming themselves, safe from the elements, I was bruised, sweaty, and nearly exhausted. The spiritual umbrella is the same way: the umbrella man must erect the umbrella in what often seems like a hurricane. In the process, the one who leads *is* going to feel bruised, sweaty, and nearly exhausted. A leader like that really does a service for others. In no way is spiritual leadership a power play.

The problem is that watching a spiritual leader at work is like watching a football team on the line of scrimmage. Unless you have played on the line in football, you really do not know what goes on there in the trenches. In the same way, those who have not borne the weight of the big umbrella, who have not shared in the responsibility of leading the church, cannot really understand what the umbrella man does.

Those who are called upon to lead must not apologize for their calling, nor should they ever abandon their responsibility because of peer pressure. God calls His pastors into the ministry and sets them aside for specific work, just as He did Paul and Barnabas. Most pastors exercise too little authority, not too much.

I have talked with hundreds of pastors who struggle with their style of ministry. My counsel is always the same: do not copy anyone else and do not succumb to peer pressure. Be God's man! Be yourself! But do be an umbrella man. Be sure that you are fulfilling your calling to be a servant to the church. Make sure your ministry provides for and makes room for the ministry of others.

The Umbrella Man as Shepherd

In his leadership, the umbrella man is also a shepherd. He must feed and care for the flock of God. He must make very sure that the spiritual feeding of the flock is first and foremost on his agenda, not earning a call to a larger church or being invited back to seminary to speak. When our Lord told Peter, "Feed My lambs. . . . Tend My sheep. . . . Feed My sheep," (John 21:15–17), He was commissioning Peter and all who are shepherds to preach and teach the Word of God faithfully. A flock cannot be gathered unless it is fed. New lambs will not be born. In short, there will be no one to lead.

Pastors who rely only on traditional programs to keep things going will neglect their preparation for preaching. By traditional I mean all of the nonessential activities that pastors are called upon to do. The shepherd, charged with feeding the sheep, is often so busy installing officers, attending luncheons, and presiding at unnecessary committee meetings that he has no time to take in spiritual food for himself so that he might feed others. I am happy to share duties with the staff such as handling weddings, social activities, business affairs, and counseling. The umbrella man has to delegate these things in order to be an effective shepherd and feed the flock.

Every preacher knows about the problem of time. He has to fight for the time to be alone with God. The pastors who are known for their strong pulpit ministries have reserved time for study and preparation.

When I was starting out, an older pastor told me, "No

one else is going to presume to schedule your time for you. As a preacher, it's up to you to set your schedule and announce it so that everyone knows that you are busy with the Lord and His Word during certain hours each day." There are things that have to be attended to by the pastor. Most preachers do not have staffs to take care of emergencies and pastoral needs. But if he makes up his mind to do it, the shepherd can set aside the time he needs for feeding the flock.

There is also the need for the preacher to reaffirm constantly and even reestablish important biblical truths with the church. The first pastor of a new church is called the founding pastor. He has to lay spiritual, theological foundations. Let every preaching pastor heed the admonition of the apostle Paul. "According to the grace of God which was given to me, as a wise master builder I have laid the foundation, and another builds on it. But let each one take heed how he builds on it. For no other foundation can anyone lay than that which is laid, which is Jesus Christ" (1 Cor. 3:10–11).

The pastor needs to keep laying these spiritual foundations, but he must be careful to build on the original apostolic foundation. The church has to be strengthened and repaired at times. This is so because spiritual truths have a way of being forgotten; spiritual foundations can become unstuck.

One pastor had worked hard to teach the basic doctrines and establish his umbrella. But he made the mistake of assuming that because he had covered the material once, he could go on to other things. In this case, the shepherd failed to provide a balanced diet to the flock. He failed to take into account three obvious facts: 1. People forget. We are all sinners and need constant reminding. 2. New people coming in have not heard what was said before. In metropolitan areas people are mobile. In such cases, manning the pulpit is like preaching to a procession. 3. Things have a way of self-destructing. You have to keep at the job of laying biblical foundations; you have to keep the umbrella erect.

A shepherd must value highly his call to preach. If he understands the implications of the call and the tremendous responsibility placed upon him, he will let nothing and no one keep him from his work.

I met a brother preacher inside mainland China on a recent trip. By prearrangement, we met in a large Chinese city. This preacher, whom I will call John, was once arrested for preaching the gospel and had been imprisoned for eighteen years for the sake of Christ. When I met him, he had been released only a short time before.

We met with a sense of camaraderie that I have felt with only a few men in my life. Here was a modern-day Paul. His thumb on one hand was gnarled and twisted from painful torture inflicted on him while he was incarcerated. During his imprisonment, his wife divorced him and all of his property was confiscated. He had paid dearly for the privilege of preaching the Word of God. Still he was smiling and was excited about meeting a Christian brother from America.

After I left him I thought, "I will never feel sorry for myself in the ministry again. I am more determined now to preach the gospel than ever before."

Later, back in Hong Kong, I spoke with amazement about John's joy and his continued commitment to the gospel. Another Chinese friend, who had arranged the meeting, said, "When they have suffered for Jesus, they are bolder than before." John continues the work of preaching the gospel to his countrymen today.

The Umbrella Man as Overseer and Protector

While I was a student preparing for the ministry and working as an understudy for an older pastor, a man who was highly respected came to me with an unholy proposition. He was a returned missionary, and I thought that all missionaries were automatically seasoned saints. I quickly lost my childish views on that subject when the gentleman proposed that he and I unite to split the church. According to his plan, I would be the new pastor and he would assist me.

It did not take much longer than the blink of an eye to say to him, "Get thee behind me, Satan." The issue was settled before it could take root. The man left the church and went on to trouble another pastor by trying to get at his student.

Something else was settled for me that day as well. I learned that I would, as part as my calling, have to protect the flock from wolves in sheep's clothing. Paul's warning to the elders at Miletus became a warning to me. "For I know this, that after my departure savage wolves will come in among you, not sparing the flock. Also from among yourselves men will rise up, speaking perverse things, to draw away disciples after themselves" (Acts 20:29–30).

Somehow, we modern Christians have lost sight of the presence of wolves. In fact, we tend to applaud someone who leaves a church and criticizes his pastor for being gutsy or courageous. We empathize with the departed who claim to have "been set free from the bondage of that place." Christian, take care! Check the dental work. It may be you are listening to a wolverine and siding against a godly pastor.

I determined as a young assistant pastor, then, that I

would defend God's man in the pulpit unless there was obvious evidence he was contrary to God's word. I thought, "This is like it was when I was a rear seat gunner. I have to protect the man's back." From that day on, I have always tried to protect those around me in the ministry as well as pastors in other churches. Thankfully, I have been blessed in the same way, protected by those who work with me.

Pastors also should be on ready alert to protect the church against false doctrine. Obviously, the best way to do this is to preach and teach sound apostolic doctrine so the counterfeit will be obvious.

Naturally, the pastor has to be careful about what he allows others to teach to his flock. Some pastors are incredibly careless about this. I have been invited to preach in churches by pastors who did not know who I was or what I believed.

Once I was visiting a relative in another state and gladly went to worship on Sunday morning with the family. When the welcome to visitors was given in the service, the pastor announced that a visiting minister was present. He asked me to stand and invited me on the spot to preach that night. What troubled me was that he did not even know my name. He did not know what I believed, but I was invited and even urged to preach.

The overseer must protect the congregation by carefully screening those who are to preach in the church he serves. I never ask anyone to preach unless he is either well-known to me or to other members of our pastoral staff.

The Umbrella Man as Equipper

The pastors who attempt to do everything alone instead of equipping others to be genuine participants in the body of Christ are making one colossal mistake. God has not called us to operate like frustrated musicians trying to play one-man bands. He has called us to an equipping ministry.

Some pastors who make the mistake of doing everything for everybody do so innocently. The habit sometimes starts at the beginning of their ministries because there is no one to share the work load. Then, by the time help arrives, the do-it-yourself pattern has been established. Others try to do everything because they think it is expected of them. But what God expects of spiritual leaders in His church is that they equip others for life and spiritual service. This is why the apostle Paul offers the instruction in Ephesians 4:11–12 which says, "And He Himself gave some to be apostles, some prophets, some evangelists, and some pastors and teachers, for the equipping of the saints for the work of ministry, for the edifying of the body of Christ."

Discipling cannot be left to the Sunday school teacher or to preaching and teaching from the pulpit alone. Discipling believers to equip them for service requires personal involvement, with concentrated feeding and required accountability. Failure in this regard explains the failure of countless churches.

The Umbrella Man as Provider of Opportunities

With the need for equipping, there is an equally important need to provide opportunities for service. If the pastor is an umbrella man, the potential for service opportunities in the church will be great. The smaller umbrellas under the big umbrella are actually ministries that can be developed. Each will need workers. Start with the children's department. If God's people can be helped to see the opportunities for service with children and be given an opportunity for training, they will serve.

The next question is, How much should the pastor let other people do? Because I see myself as an umbrella man, I can delegate to others many of the things I had to do myself in the beginning. Delegation for me means I give over certain responsibilities to others with appropriate authority to do them but I am still accountable for the outcome. Holding up the big umbrella is my primary function. Thus, I both equip others and provide opportunities for them to serve; they help me preach, baptize, conduct weddings and funerals, and all of the ministry functions. As an umbrella man, I enjoy the participation and fellowship of a ministry team. But I keep a firm hand on the umbrella.

This same philosophy works its way through the whole organization. Umbrella men, whether they hold the big umbrella or smaller ministry umbrellas underneath, are responsible to give opportunities for service under their areas of authority. Again, my task is to equip these people for service and to provide opportunities for them to serve. I will never work myself out of a job. Instead, the umbrella keeps getting bigger, and my opportunities for service keep increasing.

CHAPTER · THREE

Setting Up the Umbrella

A pastor rarely begins his ministry in a church where everything is just as it should be. The pulpit committee usually tends to paint a rosy picture in trying to interest the one they think is God's man for their church.

But this was not the case with the pulpit committee from Modesto. When they first talked to me those many years ago, they tried to tell the whole truth—without sounding too discouraging. The facts were pretty grim. The church had been through a terribly painful and disruptive upheaval. The congregation had divided between the pastor and the youth director.

Looking back on it now, the church members who were there see it as a time of spiritual warfare unparalleled in their Christian experiences. Actually, no one talks about it anymore. People do not want to remember it! I mention it here as a way of helping other pastors who might be facing the same painful ordeal. Both the pastor and the youth director left, but there were deep scars on the congregation.

I went to Modesto only because I was absolutely certain of God's call. Once there, I knew there was a huge battle to be won if the church was going to recover and grow. There were four major steps to be taken.

One: A Prophetic Pulpit

It is difficult to preach in a place where spiritual warfare has been going on and the devil has won big. When God's people go to war in the church, it is just like any other war; strategies are devised, sides are drawn, and battles are fought. Some of the battles in church wars are fought in business meetings. Other battles are waged in living rooms, restaurants, and on the phone. People get used to saying things and doing things they would otherwise never say or do. Such is war, and the wounds are deep.

But the war in Modesto was over. Eighteen months had passed since the pastor before me had left, and the leaders of the church had worked hard together and prayed fervently that peace would reign as the new man arrived to take up the work of the gospel. There I was. With ten years in the pastorate behind me, I began to preach to my new charge.

Strife had quenched the fullness of the Spirit in most of the people. There was little, if any, joy to be shared. I noticed that people did not smile much. There was tension in the air at every gathering, especially on Sundays in the sanctuary. Spiritual transmitters were jammed. Preaching was difficult in that atmosphere, but I began prayerfully.

My first sermon was appropriately titled "The Beginning." In spite of how bad things seemed, Barbara and I believed God was going to do something good for His church in Modesto. The text was Acts 2 and the sermon included some elements of Peter's first sermon. It honestly was not a very good sermon, but as the title suggested it was a beginning for us. There were times after that—many of them—when I was discouraged and not very hopeful. But the assurance of God's call kept His servants at their posts, when everything else said cut and run.

As I continued preaching from week to week, I noticed fellowship did not get easier as I had expected it would. There was a growing resistance in many people that was hard to overcome—something almost impossible to describe to anyone who has not faced it. The lack of joy became even more apparent. I wondered if I could loosen up the people with humor. But they did not smile. In fact, they showed almost no expression during worship. It was as though nobody was home.

It was then that I understood there was a problem deeper than merely poor facial expressions and lack of joy. There was a demonic kind of atmosphere that hinders even the most forceful preachers. It was extremely difficult to endure. But I kept preaching, praying, and working at what had become the battle of the pulpit.

Finally a break came. A woman came to me and announced that she was leaving. "I am afraid of you" was her reason. Sometime later I learned that she was involved in spiritism. She consulted mediums and brought their influence into the church. Having discovered this, I was glad I had not asked her to stay. She left quietly, and the next Sunday the atmosphere was better. But a pall still hung over the congregation.

Then, after about two months, another woman came to me, this time bursting into my little office to begin what quickly became a tirade. She let me know in no vague terms that I was not the pastor she wanted for her church. She said, "You are not the man for this job. I don't want you here. I am very disturbed that you came."

Then she said the magic words, "I didn't vote for you, but I didn't vote against you."

What the woman did not know, of course, was that I had not wanted to come to her church in the first place. On the night when the congregation voted for our call, Barbara and I and the children walked across the street to the motel and waited there. I had preached both morning and evening prior to the church's vote. But I wanted out.

So as we walked, I prayed silently to God, "Dear God, I don't want to come here. I'll tell you what. If there is one no vote I won't come. Amen."

Within minutes after we arrived back in our motel room, the men of the church came to tell us of the call. When I asked how the vote went, they said, "It is unanimous."

Then I asked, "Was the unanimous vote on the first or second ballot?" I thought they might have voted twice to make it unanimous.

"We only voted once. There were no negative votes." I was to be their pastor.

The two youngest children in our family screamed, "Yeah! Daddy won the election!" But I was not overjoyed. I was surprised, however, because the church had not voted with unity like that in years.

I told the woman who had come to complain how the vote had convinced me of God's call. Then I said, "If you had voted your conscience, I wouldn't be here." She too left the church, and with her leaving the preaching again became easier. Slowly, surely, in a sort of back-door revival, the breakthrough I was praying for was coming.

But I kept running into people who were plagued with unresolved anger—often vented on me. Coming into a situation where there had been this much trouble was absolutely a new experience for me. I began to wonder to whom I was preaching. Was the pulpit committee representative of the rest of the church? I began to ask, Who is listening?

There seemed to be several factions in the church, and it was difficult to tell where the people were. I knew there were many solid, Bible-believing, committed Christians in the congregation. How much of their lack of response was from broken spirits and how much was from unbelief? I decided on a plan to find out.

During the first summer of my ministry, I taught the combined adult Sunday school classes. I took an early vacation and stayed right through the summer to work with the people as much as I could in a teaching ministry. Although I had no training in poll taking, it was not difficult to develop a question-and-answer sheet each week to see if I could determine what the people's viewpoints were during those confused times.

It was 1968, and there were many issues at hand: Vietnam, the drug scene, the generation gap, police brutality, and civil rights. So in addition to questions about what the people believed about Christ and His Word, I also asked questions related to these concerns. Boxes were placed at the end of each question to check yes or no. The questions seem out of date now, but in 1968 they were matters that were on the front burner of our culture.

1. Do you believe the Bible is the actual inspired Word of God?

2. Is "police brutality" a major concern for you?

3. Is your primary concern social issues?

4. Should young men avoid the draft and go to Canada?

5. Is Jesus Christ actually God in the flesh?

After six weeks of poll taking I found that, for the most part, the congregation was made up of sincere believers who were solid in their faith in Christ and at the same time concerned about social issues. They were troubled by the Vietnam War, for example, and seemed to think we should either win or get out.

My poll also showed there were seven or eight people who seemed to be on the extreme left. They mostly were interested in political issues and, according to their answers, did not believe the Bible to be the Word of God. Their views on the person of Christ likewise were opposed to the thinking of the rest of the church. On the extreme right, there were other people who took a militant, conservative position on almost everything.

On the basis of the polls, I decided to ignore the extremes and deal with the 98 percent of the people in the center. They were, after all, the sheep to whom I was called. I could have overreacted to some of the vocal statements from the extremes, especially from the left. But I chose instead to preach the gospel and relate the Scripture to the problems of the vast majority. A running battle with the dissidents could have sunk the ship before it got out of the harbor.

If the preacher is busy reacting to what others say and do, he will never get his umbrella up. He will not be an umbrella man. He will be more like a skeet shooter, waiting for the next target to go up. This is where the little saying "Act and don't react" became my guiding light.

My advice to fellow preachers in similar situations is that they listen to their people and then wisely continue to preach the Word of God according to actual needs. The preacher should not ignore those who oppose him, but he should not adjust the gospel to them, either. Paul wrote to the problem people in Corinth of his determination to keep a steady course: "For Jews request a sign, and Greeks seek after wisdom; but we preach Christ crucified, to the Jews a stumbling block and to the Greeks foolishness" (1 Cor. 1:22–23).

In these days when so much attention is given to democracy in the church, there is one thing that has to be absolutely undemocratic. The preacher has to get his message from God's Word and deliver it with the kind of power only God can give him. He must have complete faith in God's leadership as he prepares and preaches. Only then can the battle of the pulpit be won. I did not take the polls in Modesto to find out who my friends were. I took them so I would know where people needed help, correction, and encouragement.

There are churches where one cannot tell who is in charge—the sheep or the shepherd. The shepherd must be in charge, and both the shepherds and the sheep need to know that. Shepherds need to speak with holy boldness and with the voice of the prophet.

In Modesto's case I began to preach from Mark, to establish the gospel for everyone through a brief survey of the life of Jesus. That was followed by a series of sermons from Philippians called "The Ministry of Encouragement" in the hope of healing old wounds and hurts.

Soon, signs of life were beginning to show. The people sang again and worshiped with joy. The spiritual climate so necessary for worship and service was becoming favorable. One man came and said, "Pastor, I have to tell you how good it is to hear consistent preaching of the Scriptures each week. I have actually been able to feel the life coming back in me. My wife told me that she began to notice changes in me weeks ago." What the man said was, I think, typical of what others were experiencing. The pastor before me preached the Bible just as I was doing, but when the church became embroiled in warfare, the people did not hear because the Holy Spirit was grieved. Then, through prayer, preaching, and persistence, a spiritual breakthrough was being achieved.

Two: The Call for Healing

With the preaching of the Word established, it was time to unite the divided congregation so the Lord's work could go forward. I trace the beginning of renewal and progress of the Modesto congregation to a Sunday morning of prayer and forgiveness. The divisions and hurts that had split the church began to be healed that day. Out of that experience came the beginning of a new day for God's people.

A call went out for a day of repentance, forgiveness, and dedication. I announced that the next Sunday would be given to that purpose. A larger crowd than usual gathered and at the close of a sermon on repentance, I invited all to join me in prayer at the front of the church to ask forgiveness of God and of one another, to come to peace at last.

The people came in large numbers. They asked God's forgiveness and rededicated themselves to Him. Joyfully, people reunited with those they had opposed in the past. There were many tears, smiles, and hugs. God richly blessed. We were on our way to spiritual victory. True, not everyone joined in, but revival began as we stood together that day with Christ in our midst.

The Lord alone can heal. But one of the great functions of spiritual leadership is to call God's people to repentance, and thus fulfill the ministry of reconciliation.

Three: Establishment of Priorities

Objectives, goals, and priorities have to be established in order for the church to develop. If the purpose of the church is to glorify Christ on earth, we have to ask ourselves how we are going to do it.

In our case, we determined the objective should include the development of an evangelical church committed to the Bible as the Word of God. Its main function would be to worship God, to train and equip its members to evangelize and disciple others, and to focus the outcome of the local ministry on world outreach, or missions.

This work was begun through a planning group called the Committee of the Future. Even the name gave us the feeling we were dealing with the church's destiny. The committee set a termination date, lest we would become the permanent brain trust for the church. The members were few: myself as pastor, one ministerial staff member, and three carefully chosen lay leaders. We met for six weeks. Through our efforts and much discussion and prayer, the plan was devised which is now the program of the church.

In addition to firming up our purpose, we developed

a list of priorities—the most important tasks to be done to reach the objectives. This was a first-things-first list in order of importance.

The first priority was evangelism. We put evangelism first because, although it is a part of discipleship, evangelism does not happen unless it is kept on the front burner. We wanted to make evangelism so central to the life of the church that every church member would both know of his responsibility to witness and be equipped to go about it. With this priority set, the goal of winning others to Christ was kept in view when any new program was developed. That helped keep the entire church on the same track.

Our second priority was discipleship. This meant we would major in teaching, training, and equipping believers for ministry. In the beginning, the scope of the home Bible study program and the work of accountability groups was a part of the plan, but I had no idea how important that kind of discipleship would become. Virtually everyone in leadership under the big umbrella would be discipled. Chapter 10 describes some of this work in detail.

Our next priorities were staff, program, and facilities. In looking at other congregations around the country, we found that those churches whose buildings were a top priority tended to have problems. These churches had their buildings to be sure but were lacking in staff and effective programs other than the typical Sunday schools. We decided to build both professional and lay staffs. Around them we could develop programs to accomplish our higher priorities. *Then* we included the building of facilities, but only when we would actually need them.

Al Broom was a businessman in the church. He

agreed to come on staff as business administrator to free me for other work. Soon, William H. Stewart joined the staff as youth minister. Bill was an experienced youth pastor whom I had known in Southern California. Before long, the priorities of evangelism and discipleship began to produce large numbers of young people in the church. The decision to build the professional staff first really paid off. Work was going on with adults, but the youth ministry began to fill up the evening service. The joy and excitement of that ministry to the kids in our community helped raise the umbrella higher and wider.

It is not enough, by the way, to attract a crowd of young people. Leadership must know how to disciple them and get them into evangelism. The evening service went from fifty to three hundred in the first year. Soon the morning service was overflowing, and we went to two morning services. Before long, we added a second evening service. The sanctuary, built to hold six hundred, was remodeled so that eight hundred could crowd in. Staff was added as we grew, and lay leaders were trained.

We reasoned that every time we used the sanctuary a second time on Sunday we were getting a free building. So instead of adding to the building, we kept on adding staff and using the building over again. Then, when we went to the third Sunday morning service, making five for the day, Ron Blanc came on staff as my preaching partner.

Using the existing building until we actually were turning people away was good medicine. Those who opposed what we were doing could not fight success. And the people who were happily involved were beginning to say, "Pastor, we have to build some new buildings." Thus people were not only ready to build but were willing to give sacrificially for that purpose.

Starting with staff and programs built around the staff, while using our existing facilities to the utmost, gave us great motivation. It was like taxiing an airplane to the end of the runway, revving up the engines with the brakes locked, and then letting it go at full power. Now that we had the staff, the program, and the people, we needed a new auditorium. That was how our priorities worked for us in getting the umbrella up to its maximum effectiveness.

Four: Dealing with Decay

The final step in setting up the umbrella has to do with being wise as serpents, harmless as doves. What is the best way to deal with those who oppose what you are trying to do? Let me explain what we did. Our way is not the only way, and things do not always work out as well as our situation did, but I think it is the best way.

When Jesus sent out the twelve on a preaching mission, He said to them, "Behold, I send you out as sheep in the midst of wolves. Therefore be wise as serpents and harmless as doves" (Matt. 10:16). The serpent is a symbol of intellectual perception, shrewdness, and wisdom. The dove is the symbol of innocence and single-mindedness. The disciple of the Lord is not to be naive and simplistic but is to look at the heart of a problem. He is called to use wisdom in gaining victories for his Lord. But in his shrewdness, he is never to succumb to expediency and underhanded ways. It is crucial to follow Christ's instruction when setting up the umbrella for ministry.

There is a tendency for leaders in the church, who have been in office for a long time, to say those unfortunate seven last words of the church, which are "We have always done it this way." I spent most of my time in the first years of the Modesto ministry sitting down with people over coffee or at lunch and explaining why we needed to do things differently.

Before I ever accepted the call to Modesto, the church agreed to shift to the one-board system of government. When the time came to adopt the new constitution and bylaws, an older gentleman stood in the congregational meeting to oppose the issue, claiming to represent a large segment of the congregation. The motion passed without difficulty, but I determined to meet with him and get him involved in the process before the church's next important meeting. I invited him to lunch the next week.

As we sat down, I told him I was interested in his opinion; that I wanted to get his views on what needed to be done in the future. I explained that the time soon was coming to establish the priorities of the church's ministry. This conciliatory meeting was arranged in the hope of enlisting him as a helper. Though time-consuming, it was far more desirable than seeing him always unhappy and objecting. I laid out the plans I had in mind, and I told him about priorities of evangelism and discipleship, plus other things ahead. He talked thoughtfully about each item brought up for discussion. Finally, he struck the table with a loud slap and exclaimed, "Pastor, we can do it!"

My meetings with other outspoken members of the flock in those early days were not always that enjoyable, nor were they so happily concluded. But face-to-face conferences over lunch helped these people become a part of the process of change. These were not enemies of the faith at all, but rather people who needed to be shown consideration and given a chance to offer their opinions. It was a small price to pay for the making of friends who enlisted as supporters and builders of the church instead of critics.

Let me state it bluntly: intimidation by church members is one of the basic causes for the failures of many pastors. When a member shows aggression against the pastor, it is important that the shepherd knows he is called to the Lord's work *where he is*. He must understand that spiritual warfare is real and unending. He must be prepared to meet all kinds of attacks, even from the most unlikely sources.

Several times in those first weeks and months at the church, people who were still angry at the former pastor transferred their anger to me. It seemed strange that on several occasions elderly women in church came at me with verbal barrages they apparently never were able to fire off at him. Fortunately, God opened my eyes to their frustrations and the attacks did not bother me. But there were times when I had to stop them and explain that I was their pastor now and they were not to talk to me like that. God had sent me to them. Those were incredibly important words. It was as though they had not realized what they were saying. In every case (there were five) they repented, and we became friends.

When you are working to set up the spiritual umbrella and create, with God's help and power, a wholesome, friendly, spiritual environment in the church, the umbrella you hold can become a lightning rod. The one who is setting up a spiritual umbrella is going to be challenged. He often is opposed, discouraged, and intimidated by the efforts of a few who want to control the church.

For them, the name of the game is *power*. Such people do not want to see change. They want, instead, to be in charge. This is where the leader serves the common good of the church by exercising his leadership. Yet, more pastors are lost because of intimidation from church bullies than for any other reason. The pastor who sets out to establish a spiritual canopy does so at his own risk. He must learn how to handle aggression without being intimidated and without becoming an aggressor himself.

Often a challenge comes from an informal leader, or one who exerts leadership although he is not an officeholder. His strength may be his winning personality. A young pastor friend of mine discovered one such enemy of Christ the hard way. As spiritual progress became evident under his preaching, a man who had been vocal and forceful in the church for years began to oppose the young pastor. Predictably, he was not on the official board, but a leader by virtue of his charisma.

From veiled complaints, the attacks increased to full-scale intimidation. Finally, he made a direct verbal attack on both the pastor and his wife. There is an old saying, "You can tell a wolf in sheep's clothing because wolves eat lambs."

In his role as wolf—and he was a wolf—he took the unsuspecting pastoral couple aside at a social gathering. There, he blasted them with accusations about their marriage, their calling, and their work in the church. Deeply shocked and hurt, they spent several sleepless nights agonizing about whether to resign from the ministry and leave the church.

But after prayer and counsel, they were alerted to their accuser's base intention to intimidate the shepherd and run him off. In the light of day, and with prayer, even wolves do not look so strong. The young pastor took his case directly to the church board. The elders were outraged that such an attack had been made on the pastor and his wife. One board member recalled the Scripture "Do not receive an accusation against an elder except from two or three witnesses" (1 Tim. 5:19). Obviously, this injunction had been violated. The accuser was rebuked.

The battle, however, was not over. He stood his ground. At a congregational meeting, the assailant demanded the pastor's resignation. At that moment a church member stood up and said, "Wait a minute! Who gave you the right to tell my pastor to leave?" It was an example of how thoughtful, God-fearing Christians love and defend their pastors—if they understand the situation. The accuser left the church. The pastor stayed and the church grew.

Most men called to serve the Lord are tenderhearted and sensitive. When criticism and opposition come, in their humility they often will consider them valid, thinking the accusers see something they do not.

A pastor must listen to everyone in his flock and learn to take both praise and criticism gracefully. But the pastor must not be intimidated! Neither must he be paranoid and see every person with a problem as an enemy. He must keep his discernment and minister to the flock. Then, when trouble comes—and it will—the pastor must be a man of faith and stay with the sheep. Getting the umbrella up is no job for the fainthearted.

The Nature of Spiritual Leadership

When the term *strong leadership* is used today, eyebrows go up. "Hey, nobody tells me what to do," comes one objection. Perhaps even the cry of "dictator" is raised.

The problem is that we have failed to realize a spiritual leader *must* be strong. If he or she is anointed by God for a particular ministry, the very power of God will be at work in and through that person. Yet, modern believers often are troubled by the very idea that someone in charge of the spiritual fold might be strong. There is a subtle patriphobia (fear of a father) at work. It is as though only God Himself should be strong and all of His anointed should be weak!

This is not the case in biblical history, nor is it to be the case in the church today. So much has been said about nondirective leadership styles that the genuine leadership of godly men often is misinterpreted. "Jim Jones," some muse to themselves, "authoritarian." A strong leader is thought of as a hard-nosed person set in concrete, a tyrant who forces his way on others. Let us take a good look at what constitutes genuine strength in a Christian leader.

Defining Our Terms

The word *strong* often is misunderstood because most of us associate it with power in the world. For us, strength means political power, muscle power, ability to intimidate and to bully, or authority to command. And all this comes in a period of history when the mood is nobody tells anybody else what to do.

In reality, when we talk about spiritual leadership, we are talking about spiritual authority that comes from being the first among equals. So a strong spiritual leader in this book is one who is called and gifted by God to an office within the church. God blesses such leadership, for a strong spiritual leader is told to exhibit qualities similar to those of Jesus Christ. Jesus was a strong leader; people still are following Him nearly two thousand years later. But He went about His leadership in a rather quiet way. His strength was not like that of world leaders. It is Jesus' quiet quality of leadership that we are talking about. This quiet strength in spiritual leadership is precisely what our modern church needs.

In order to examine the nature of spiritual leadership we must answer three questions.

1. Is the leader accountable and to whom?
2. Is he responsible and does he act responsibly?
3. Can he handle authority without becoming authoritarian?

Accountability

Accountability is the first question raised when leadership is discussed. To whom does the leader report? When asked that question, most spiritual leaders will answer, "I am accountable to God." But that answer by itself is not acceptable. It is too simplistic, because *everybody* ultimately reports to God. That is what the judgment seat of Christ is all about. What I want to know is, to whom do we answer among ourselves?

We can clear things up somewhat if we note that there is a vast difference between saying generally "I am accountable to God" and saying more specifically "I make myself accountable to God each day in prayer." Everybody is accountable on the last day, but not everybody is answering to God each day for his actions. Inevitably, the one who is not giving account to God daily will hedge when asked about his prayer life: "No, I don't have a regular time; I pray all through the day." It may be that some can make that work, but if one is to make himself accountable to God in prayer, he must do so regularly.

The spiritual leader is accountable in other ways, also. In the episcopal polity of the large church bodies such as the Roman, Orthodox, Anglican, Lutheran, and Methodist churches, pastors are directly accountable to bishops who oversee their work. The bishops, in turn, report to councils or synods.

In the absence of such hierarchy in many evangelical churches, pastors in a number of cities are entering into accountability groups with one another, asking for accountability and spiritual direction to one another. Similarly, throughout most of church history, pastors had spiritual directors, those who would give them guidance in godly matters.

Is there a biblical basis for such accountability? Recall that in Galatians 2, the apostle Paul submitted his ministry to the oversight of Peter, James, and John years after his conversion on the road to Damascus to make sure he was not "running in vain." In the same way, men like Timothy and Titus took direction from Paul. And both these men, in turn, established elders in the churches. We actually find no biblical support for those who insist upon independence and refusal to submit to authority.

There is a more subtle sort of accountability that offers oversight for the Christian leader. He is accountable to his wife. It is very clear that a husband and wife are accountable to each other for their sex life. In writing to the Corinthians Paul said, "The wife does not have authority over her own body, but the husband does. And likewise the husband does not have authority over his own body, but the wife does" (1 Cor. 7:4). This must apply especially to spiritual leaders who are called upon to set good examples as heads of families.

While being head of his home, the spiritual leader is accountable to his wife in virtually every way. He must be before her what he presents himself to be in front of the church. With her he has to be genuine. She will know him for what he really is. The same is true for his relationship with his children. The son of a spiritual leader who says "My dad is a phony" and means it is either angry at his father and getting even or he has witnessed a great hypocrisy. The spiritual leader is accountable in his home.

Paul writes about how he and Barnabas were being treated. "Do we have no right to take along a believing wife, as do also the other apostles, the brothers of the Lord, and Cephas?" (1 Cor. 9:5). Note here that the other men of God did not leave their wives behind. The wives were with their husbands in the ministry. I believe the couples were together not only to meet each other's needs, but to witness that their homes were in order.

The spiritual leader must also be accountable to those

he leads. In some cases, congregations vote on their pastor's call to the church on a yearly basis, while others review the call every three years. This practice is not designed to make the leadership of the pastor tentative. Instead it says that the pastor is accountable for his handling of the Scriptures, for his theology, and for his conduct as a minister of the gospel. He must be free to preach as God leads him, so that he truly can be God's man. He must speak to the church to make everyone accountable to God. But if he veers from the truth and his life is not consistent with his calling and profession of faith, he will be held accountable before the congregation.

In my case, I am obligated to comply with and enthusiastically support the decisions made by the church's official board. This is often the situation in churches with congregational government. I participate in both the decision-making process and the execution of the decisions.

But making myself accountable to the official board that governs the church does not mean they are the shepherds and I the sheep. Board members are not authorized to supervise the pastor's work and lead him around at will. I cannot imagine the original seven deacons keeping watch on Peter. I rather think it was the other way around. The accountability of pastors should be a system of checks and balances against something serious—incompetency, ineffectiveness, irresponsibility, or immorality—not the running of his ministry.

Responsibility

The next question to consider is responsibility. The one called to lead the church must not only be accountable, he or she must be responsible. I want to point out the need both to be responsible and to act responsibly. To be responsible means the leader must be willing to bear the burden for the success or the failure of the undertaking upon his shoulders. President Harry Truman made the saying "The buck stops here" famous when he was called upon to make some momentous decisions at the close of World War II. Regardless of how Harry Truman is remembered, his willingness to take blame or praise for his action was the hallmark of a good leader.

Furthermore, this willingness to bear responsibility is a Christlike quality in a Christian leader and should be looked upon as a key to serving Christ and His church. Such leaders often are praised for the good work done, but few people actually see the other side of that coin. Criticism and complaints are often the lot of the one who leads and bears responsibility. When Jesus said "Whoever desires to come after Me, let him deny himself, and take up his cross, and follow Me" (Mark 8:34), He was talking at least in part about pastoral leaders in the church. Those who are willing to bear responsibility are strong leaders. Being responsible is at the heart of spiritual leadership, but it is the same with any kind of leadership. A leader who is unwilling to be responsible is no leader at all.

Being responsible is fulfilling an obligation. Paul felt obligation when he said to the Romans, "I am a debtor both to Greeks and to barbarians, both to wise and to unwise. So, as much as is in me, I am ready to preach the gospel to you who are in Rome also" (Rom. 1:14–15). Having received the gospel, Paul felt the obligation to preach it wherever he could.

Those who, like Paul, feel this obligation are not likely to look for comfy jobs in prestigious places. The pastor who seeks success in the typical worldly way might be like a hireling. He does well in building up the church. He is a good preacher and works hard at getting people motivated and involved. As the church begins to grow, he may lead a building program to care for the new people coming in. But then to everyone's dismay, Dr. Successful accepts a call to a larger church in another city, leaving the people to carry on by themselves, hoping to find new leadership.

Some would say, "Wait a minute, the man had to listen to God's calling." This is true. But does God always call his servants to bigger churches and more income? Every call of God to His pastors is a case-by-case matter. But those who have good ministry skills and are successful church builders are not necessarily strong leaders. To be strong in the Lord, one must be a responsible shepherd who can say no to new Buicks and bigger bucks for the sake of his sheep.

Some of God's most responsible shepherds serve in obscure places and are not known either as strong leaders or for their work in the ministry. But there is great strength in those who commit themselves to God's people and give their lives to their work.

I once visited the old leper colony on the island of Molokai in the Hawaiian Islands. There, Father Damien served the lepers for over fifty years. He committed himself *for life* to help those with that dreaded disease. In the end, he contracted leprosy himself and died among the lepers he served.

A strong leader will make a strong commitment because he takes his responsibility seriously. He wisely knows he cannot ask God's people to commit themselves to the work of Christ if he is not committed to them. He must be able to say "I am willing to be here with you for the rest of my life" and mean it. If the Lord calls him away, he must of course go. But he should not be looking for something better.

To act responsibly, then, is "to have a walk worthy of the calling with which you were called" (Eph. 4:1). This means that spiritual leadership must be principled, not expedient. Christians everywhere, but especially spiritual leaders, must do what is right, no matter the cost. To be principled means to follow the instructions and commandments of God and live moral and upright lives.

Expediency, also called Machiavellianism, says, "Let the end justify the means." If your goal is important, do whatever you have to do to get there. This is the world's way of looking at values. Expediency gets the job done, no matter how many bodies are strewn in the path.

A pastor or Bible teacher is using expediency if he attempts to teach what he has not first studied. A Christian businessman is following the expedient way if he advertises one product and substitutes another without notice. A finance committee is practicing expediency if it collects funds for one purpose and uses them for another. A Christian chooses the expedient way when he tells a lie.

Sadly, many Christian leaders have followed the ways of the world in this regard rather than the way of Christ. Spiritual leadership that is principled will be scrupulously honest in all matters. To be unfaithful in one way is to set the stage for unfaithfulness in others.

There is a crying need in the church for leaders who will be responsible and act responsibly. We should be able to say with Paul, "But we have renounced the hidden things of shame, not walking in craftiness nor handling the word of God deceitfully, but by manifestation of the truth commending ourselves to every man's conscience in the sight of God" (2 Cor. 4:2).

Authority Versus Authoritarianism

The next question is "Can he handle authority without becoming authoritative?" The answer will depend to a great extent upon how he interprets his calling from God. In recent years it has been the practice of some to minimize the importance of God's calling on an individual's life. The one called by God may never see a burning bush, but he had better know that he is on holy ground. The call may be received in a different way for each person, but when the call to ministry comes it should be unmistakably clear and life-changing.

When a pastor is called to lead a church, he must assume responsibility and spiritual authority there. Paul was very emphatic about his assigned responsibility and authority with the Corinthians. He spelled it out for them this way: "We, however, will not boast beyond measure, but within the limits of the sphere which God appointed us—a sphere which especially includes you" (2 Cor. 10:13).

It is clear that God assigns pastors and other spiritual leaders to specific works. If that is not so, let us stop talking about the "calling of God." Peter spoke of such an assignment when he urged pastors to be examples to the flock. The words "entrusted to you" in 1 Peter 5:3 actually mean that these members of the flock in the church are individually allotted to the pastor's care. The word used in the original is the word for the "lot" in the casting of lots. If the pastor truly understands that his call to the pastorate is a call to care for sheep that belong to the Chief Shepherd, he can handle authority without becoming authoritative. He must lead the sheep and not drive them. He must lead without ownership.

The writer to the Hebrews goes further and warns that the shepherds must give account for those in their charge. The verse which often is quoted by leaders but seldom read in churches says: "Obey those who rule over you and be submissive, for they watch out for your souls, as those who must give account. Let them do so with joy and not with grief, for that would be unprofitable for you" (Heb. 13:17).

The point I must make is this: it is inconceivable that there would be no authority given to accompany the great responsibility laid upon pastors and spiritual leaders by God. If I must give an accounting to God for the members of the flock, I must have something to say about what is going on in the church. It is easy for those who do not bear such great responsibility to complain about a pastor's supposed authority. Their names are not on the contract. Still, I have to handle that responsibility and authority as a sacred trust, answerable in all things to God.

The pastor's authority is actually in the Word of God. This is why I said in Chapter 3 that shepherds have to be in charge. Paul was using his authority when he said, "What do you want? Shall I come to you with a rod, or in love and a spirit of gentleness?" (1 Cor. 4:21). The rod he spoke of was the Word of God.

So it is that the power evidenced in a pastor's preaching will indicate how much influence he will have in church leadership. If he faithfully and skillfully preaches and teaches the Scriptures, God's people will look to him for leadership in other areas. It becomes apparent that because God has entrusted him with the sacred Word he can be trusted to lead the church in all matters.

Strangely, although he does not command the church, the pastor is responsible for its care. His leadership must be by influence. He helps people to see what must be done, but they must do it voluntarily. Therefore, the members must see by what he says and what he does that he is God's man. They will follow him if they know that. This is another way of saying that he leads by example.

In Matthew 23:11–12, Jesus warned against the Pharisees who loved the high places at feasts and synagogues. They were religious superstars who claimed prestigious titles, natural men making supernatural claims. He said, "But he who is greatest among you shall be your servant. And whoever exalts himself will be abased, and he who humbles himself will be exalted." James 4:6 adds to this and says, "God resists the proud, but gives grace to the humble." Our Lord was not saying there should be no leaders! He was saying leaders must be servants. They must be humble people.

Sometimes things are not the way they seem. The spiritual leader who is not truly humble may appear strong when in reality he is weak. The same is true for the leader walking in humility. He may appear to be weak to those around him, but he is strong in the Lord. Remember that humility is not primarily behavior, but identity and attitude. It is not acting humble. It is being free and strong. Let us look at some pastors who do not understand true humility. Perhaps we can all see some of ourselves in these sketches.

Commander Cody

"Commander Cody" is the type of leader who always expects to be in full control of everything. He is power oriented. He hesitates to take counsel from anyone.

Conceiving a plan of action, he manipulates others to get the votes or support he needs for his project. He sees himself as the focus of attention and is a master at convincing others to give him center stage. His style of leadership requires that he make all the decisions. When he is away from the church, all work grinds to a halt because nothing can be done without his approval.

The obvious flaw in this type of ministry is that it is limited to one man's span of control. He is unwilling to delegate authority and responsibility. The result is a ministry stifled by an overbearing personality.

Chicken Charlie

"Chicken Charlie" is the leader who is afraid of competition that capable and talented coworkers might give him. His fears stem from feelings of incompetence brought about by (1) a lack of training, (2) limited skills, (3) a poor self-image, and (4) a weak spiritual life.

How can you identify him? He surrounds himself with others less capable than himself. Because the praise of others is very important to him, he is careful that no one with whom he is involved could be a threat to his self-esteem. He cannot help anyone else learn to minister successfully, for he has never learned himself that the key to successful ministry is a humble spirit. Chicken Charlie's entire life consists of continual self-evaluations and weak attempts to defend his sagging ego.

What is the answer to Charlie's problem? He must discover the liberating power of humility. If he has a lack of skills or poor training, he will then have the freedom to learn from others.

Praise from men no longer will be as crucial as before. Best of all, he will be able to allow others to minister and will rejoice with them rather than see them as possible threats.

E. Frederick Fakeout

"E. Frederick Fakeout" is the spiritual leader who presents himself as a great scholar. In reality, he is essentially a copier and collector of other men's thoughts. While there is nothing wrong in learning from others, Dr. Fakeout never gives credit where credit is due. "Borrowing from one source is plagiarism; borrowing from many sources is *research*," he reminds his critics at the quarterly ministerium. Like Cody and Charlie, E. Frederick is busy seeking the praise of men—but with him it takes on a decidedly intellectual bent.

E. Frederick is a product of the competition from television, radio, tape ministries, and local preaching contests. In an effort to keep up with this intense competition, E. Frederick works on his speaking voice, shops expensive men's store sales, and pretends to be something he is not. Although Dr. Fakeout is very good at the game he plays, sooner or later people will figure him out. The remedy for E. Frederic Fakeout is what he calls *metanoia* (repentance), some hard work, and a true understanding of what it means to be a servant.

Showboat Sam

Showboat is a term used in the sports world for the athlete who is always showing off or grandstanding for the benefit of the fans. This spiritual leader is all show and no go. He does well in public relations and may wow the crowds with a brilliant Sunday morning performance, but a close examination of Sam's fruit shows little real discipleship or maturity among the faithful. The minister, of couse. is not to entertain his flock; he is not on stage. He is to equip the believers for the ministry. But Showboat Sam never learned this. And he will not unless he gets serious before his Lord and realizes his mission and the mission of the church.

Doormat Dan

"Doormat Dan" is the spiritual leader afraid of any opposition. The T-shirt under his Geneva gown reads "Please Tread on Me." Unwilling to take the risk that his leadership role requires, Dan lets others decide his ministry for him. The finance committee and the women's groups love him for it. He is a man who appears humble, but he is really only frightened.

There is a great difference between fear and humility. One will make you cringe while the other will make you bold. If he truly humbles himself before God, Dan will have all the boldness he needs.

The Strength of Humility

Spiritual leaders are strong when they can get themselves out of the way and really begin to care about people. A leader is strong when he can enjoy hearing others around him praised. He is strong when he rejoices as they excel in what they do. He is strong when he can praise others and seek what is best for them.

This strength is God-given. It is spiritual strength that the Holy Spirit builds into our character if we are willing. This character strength comes through humility. What is humility? Here is the definition that has helped me the most: humility is knowing who you are before God and then relating as a servant to His sovereignty.

In the New Testament, humility is seen as lowliness, but it is a relative term. It is the opposite of self-exaltation, and it rules out pride altogether. To be humble means that one sees himself as lower than the Lord, but not as insignificant! Such a person truly acknowledges the exalted Christ as his Lord. He actually and finally comes to understand and accept the sovereignty of God. When the proper relationship of servant-to-Lord is established in the heart, humility follows. Servanthood truly begins.

A young businessman was inconsistent in his spiritual life. It was not that way for him in the beginning. At first he was in high gear and excited about his new life in Christ. At every opportunity he witnessed to his friends and family. His tithe was joyfully given each week, and he was always in worship and active in church activities.

Then he began to cool down. The enthusiasm he had felt for the Lord and His church began to be directed elsewhere. Business became everything to him. He was back serving men. His tithe still came in regularly, but most often by mail. (Giving money is not always an indicator of spiritual life and vitality.) Soon he was more absent than present. This continued until finally he began to grow cold. And then he grew critical. He began to talk to others about his grievances with the church and the pastor: he had "concerns."

At that point we had a talk.

Our talk was about the sovereignty of God and the lordship of Jesus Christ. I asked him, "Is Jesus Christ the Lord of your life?"

That question brought the whole picture into focus. The young businessman look grieved. He leaned forward with his head in his hands and thought for a long time. Then slowly he said, "No, I haven't honored Jesus Christ as Lord in my life. Wait. Now I think I see what's wrong. You don't have to probe any further, pastor." There were tears at first and then joy at the new freedom he was beginning to experience.

Later the young man came to me and said with a smile, "Pastor, I am ready to be God's servant at last. Jesus Christ is really Lord of my life now. I want to serve Him." We hugged each other and, with tears, we prayed and thanked God for His victory. The man was happy because he had found himself. I rejoiced with him, but I was happy because he now was going to help me hold up the umbrella instead of fouling the spiritual climate with imagined grievances.

Through repentance we can enter into a true faith relationship with our Lord. Our identity is established at the point of faith. Just as repentance shows us who we are not, by revealing our sin to us, faith shows us who we are—children of the King. We are authenticated by faith as belonging to the living God, standing in a secure, permanent, and participating relationship with Him.

It is important to know that you are authentic. This is what happened to the apostle Paul with his "thorn in the flesh." Apparently his heavenly visions put him in danger of becoming proud, so the Lord allowed him to suffer some affliction. When Paul asked to be freed from it, God answered, "My grace is sufficient for you, for My strength is made perfect in weakness" (2 Cor. 12:9).

Conclusion

It is strange that humility often is looked upon as weakness, when it is a marvelous strength. The confusion results in trying to apply unregenerate, unspiritual thoughts to spiritual things. Humility makes one free to serve, and it provides strength of character. It is one of those quiet qualities of leadership that is required in an umbrella man. Academic and professional training can help equip the spiritual leader for service, but he has to come to know the freedom and strength that true humility brings by personal spiritual growth.

The nature of spiritual leadership is that it is strong. It is accountable and responsible. It is principled and not expedient. A strong spiritual leader can handle authority without becoming authoritative. The strength of God himself is made available to His servants when they are humble.

Centuries ago, Saint Ephraim—himself a pastor—prayed daily for humility. His prayer has lasted to this day and is rich in true servanthood.

O Lord and Master of my life, take from me the spirit of laziness, faintheartedness, lust for power, and idle talk. But give to me, your servant, a spirit of soberness, humility, patience, and love. O Lord and King, grant me to see my own faults and not to condemn my brother: for you are blessed forever and ever. Amen.

Selecting Your Leadership

An umbrella man's success will depend a great deal upon his skill and wisdom in selecting leaders. Some spiritual leaders seem to have a God-given ability to discern leadership qualities in people. Others of us struggle. Either way, an ability to select good people can be acquired by any leader who will learn what to look for and discipline himself to be objective in his choices.

The leader must learn to select prayerfully those people who not only have the required *skills* for leadership, but have the *hearts* to lead as well. We will discuss some of the criteria for selecting leaders here; the training of leaders will be dealt with in Chapter 7.

Nothing speaks of failure in a spiritual leader's ministry as does the failure to select and train other leaders. Time and again I have talked with pastors who, when they began to work in a new church, found there were virtually no trained workers on hand. When asked why, the people of the church usually said, "Our former pastor did everything." If the pastor had worked at selecting and training leaders to help him instead of doing all of the work himself, he could have expanded the ministry. And he could have prepared it for further growth under the next pastor. The church needed an umbrella man.

Another problem that should be considered is the tendency today to opt for management systems over leadership. With the development of new management theories and with the use of computers in most businesses and in many churches, the value and necessity for authentic spiritual leadership can be blurred and even lost. Remember, leadership and management, while closely related, are not the same. Leadership directs the course of events; management carries out the day-to-day functions of the organization. If the manager is the helmsman of the vessel, the leader is the captain on the bridge who sets the course. But even such analogies as this fall far short of explaining the importance of leadership in the church—or in any organization.

One of the great contributions of leadership is that it inspires. People follow the one who can inspire them to go and who can show them in a convincing way why they should go. There is a saying well-known to military leaders: "When you have to get men into a tough situation, you can't send them there, but you can take them there." In the procession from darkness to light, spiritual leaders have to "take them there."

It is also said that "You can tell a leader because others are following him." This is true, but for Christian leadership it does not go far enough. The question for the spiritual leader is "Where are you leading the ones who are following you?" The implications involved in spiritual leadership are eternal in their scope and, therefore, more important than other kinds of leadership. This is why the selection of spiritual leaders is so important.

Looking for Leaders

The United States Marine Corps advertises for people who will dedicate themselves to the defense of their country and loyalty to the corps. The slogan "We need a few good men" appeals to the pride of those enlisting. While it is true the USMC chooses comparatively few men, it also trains them intensely.

We in the church are not training mere marines; we are involved in a much greater battle. We also have a more important mission. If we think of spiritual leaders and workers as those who represent the King of kings, we are more apt to be careful in our selection of such leaders. This high view of spiritual leadership was expressed by Paul when he said, "Therefore we are ambassadors for Christ, as though God were pleading through us: we implore you on Christ's behalf, be reconciled to God" (2 Cor. 5:20).

In the church everyone is a potential leader, but everyone will not or cannot lead. We must look for those who are spiritually equipped by God and who are motivated to take on the responsibility of leadership. We will deal here with the criteria for lay leaders as well as professionals on the ministerial staff—the requirements are much the same. With that in mind, let us look at how we can locate and select those who are equipped by God to lead—and have the hearts to do it.

1. Motivated People

We begin with motivation because a candidate for spiritual leadership must want to serve God enough to take on such responsibility. He must be willing to work hard to prepare himself for the work ahead. Most ministers, for example, must take formal training in educational institutions. Then, if they are able, they will undertake an internship to become equipped for service as leaders.

In the same way, but not to the same degree, lay leaders should be willing to work and train for the responsibility they will carry. In the Modesto church, men are not selected to serve on the board of deacons, the official board, until they have completed the forty-week evangelism course. Among other requirements, they also must have completed at least one course in the home Bible study program and must have served as group leaders before they are chosen as deacons.

Why should Christian leaders be anything but highly motivated and soundly mature if they are going to serve the King of kings? It does not matter how much skill a person has. If he is not motivated to work hard and get himself ready for service, he could do more harm than good.

An athletic coach will tell you the same thing. No matter how much native ability an athlete has, if he will not practice with the team and work hard to develop his skills, he will either end up on the bench or turn in his suit. In fact, those with great skills should recognize that they have a responsibility to develop even further what God has given them.

Too often, gifted people want to ride on their gifts. They do not want to perfect their skills. Those who select leadership candidates must choose people who are willing to work hard and bear the burden of leadership.

However, people who are highly motivated are not

automatically qualified to serve as leaders. What else should we look for?

After motivation, there are at least three other absolutely vital elements to look for in selecting and training a candidate for spiritual leadership: (1) proven godliness and spiritual maturity, (2) emotional stability, and (3) spiritual gifts and abilities.

If we look for ability first, we might get someone with great skills and talents but who is fearfully lacking in the spiritual and emotional dimensions. The most glaring example of this is too often seen when a minister of music is hired. We hear him sing solos and lead the congregation in singing. We think, "What a performer! This man can make our ministry more attractive."

Unfortunately, if he is not spiritually mature and emotionally sound, he might fill the choir loft with other performers who are much like himself. The worship service will become a religious Lawrence Welk show.

Take that a step further and realize that if he is not emotionally mature, the choir loft might also become the "war department" of the church. Members who bicker and feud can quench the Holy Spirit even as they sing beautiful music. Every pastor who has ever preached with that kind of choir behind him on the platform will know what I mean.

Apologies to music ministers here! The same thing can happen in every area of service where the order of priorities is reversed. Many congregations choose pastors after hearing them preach only once. Some men are chosen for pulpits without answering questions that would establish their qualifications for the tremendously important work of preaching and leading Christ's church. In selecting any spiritual leader remember to look for proven godliness and spiritual maturity, emotional stability, and then gifts and abilities—*in that order*.

2. Proven Godliness and Spiritual Maturity

Proven godliness is a requirement for both bishops and deacons. Concerning bishops, we find in 1 Timothy 3:4 the need for the bishop to rule his own household well, "having his children in submission with all reverence." That is proven godliness, for what he has been able to do in his home, he will be able to do in the church.

We find that the candidate should have experience in the Christian life, "not a novice, lest being puffed up with pride he fall in the same condemnation as the devil," and he also "must have a good testimony among those who are outside, lest he fall into reproach and the snare of the devil" (1 Tim. 3:6–7).

Clearly, then, the leadership candidate must have a track record. He must not be a new Christian, and he must have a good reputation. What about those who have dramatic conversions, who were once criminals or drunks or drug pushers? The temptation is to exploit them and give them too much too fast. They become celebrities before they learn to become servants. That almost always ends in disaster.

Proven godliness will be accompanied by spiritual maturity. The biblical word for maturity in the original means "to be completed." Obviously none of us in this present life will be completed altogether, but certainly the one who is spiritually mature has grown in the Lord. In Hebrews 5:14 we read concerning maturity, "But solid food belongs to those who are of full age, that is, those who by reason of use have their senses exercised to discern both good and evil."

In the case of deacons, the same kind of requirements applies. In 1 Timothy 3:10, godliness is necessary for their office. "But let these also first be proved; then let them serve as deacons, being found blameless."

I look for spiritual maturity in a potential leader, whether he is to be called on the staff or to be trained as a lay leader. Ask the direct and frontal questions of a motivated candidate for leadership. Does he have a vital faith relationship with the Lord Jesus Christ? How does he care for his wife and children? If the candidate is a married woman, an appropriate question regarding her relationship with her husband and family should be asked. For candidates who are single, ask for their moral commitments to be clear. Church romances which plague the ministry would be diminished if questions about priorities and chastity are dealt with when selecting leaders. Those who do not have solid family relationships in the home should not be leaders in the church.

Is he or she a good steward of God's blessing, both material and otherwise? Does he give to God what belongs to God? And does he give to Caesar what belongs to Caesar? (see Matt. 22:21). Jesus said, "He who is faithful in what is least is faithful also in much; and he who is unjust in what is least is unjust also in much" (Luke 16:10). You can tell a lot about people's lives by how they handle money. Spiritual leaders should be paid appropriately and then be able to live within their means. They should pay their creditors. And most of all they should bring their tithes and offerings before the Lord.

Other important questions should deal with account-ability. I would want to know if the candidate is willing to be accountable to me. Would he be willing to answer to others for his actions? Most of all, does he make himself accountable to God every day in prayer? Has he the conviction that the Bible is the inspired Word of God? Is he knowledgeable in the Scriptures? I am less concerned with his position on any current, trendy theological debate. The real issue is obedience. Finally, is he a man of prayer and a witness for the Lord?

3. Emotional Stability

Emotional stability is the third critical element in selecting and training leaders. Does the candidate see himself as a *servant* of God, or does he see a possible leadership role as an *honor* bestowed upon him? If the answer is the latter, he will demand praise for his work and will think more of himself than of the people he is to serve.

One pastor told me about what happened when he failed to ascertain the answer to this vital question. He found himself working with a prima donna. He had assumed that a certain lay leader was a servant of God with a servant's heart. However, very soon the lay leader my friend had selected began to make demands for himself. He spoke of "my people," meaning those who served on his committee. And he began to speak to others about his authority. Finally he began to gather people around him, forming a political base for imagined victories in church business meetings.

Fortunately, one day he threatened to resign his important position if he did not get his way on an issue he had raised. His resignation was accepted instantly, almost before he could get it all said! The pastor now says,

"I have been looking for servants, not prima donnas, ever since."

Is the candidate living in the real world? In other words, is he mentally healthy? Although it might seem that this question would be easily answered by observation, I mention it here because I once knew an emotionally fragile pastor who became mentally ill. In his illness, he imagined that God had called him to build a bridge across the Atlantic Ocean to Europe. Peace would come if he built the bridge. I hate to say it, but what was even stranger was that some of his Christian followers thought it was a terrific idea! They defended the man against those who realized his true condition. So if you select emotionally unstable people, others like them will rally around. Then you *really* will have a problem.

There are other points to consider regarding a candidate's emotional stability. For example, does he have a critical spirit? It is one thing to be analytical, but quite another thing to be supercritical. That speaks of a deeper problem. Pride will cause some people to be critical of everything that does not originate with them.

A very important consideration linked with the problem of the critical spirit is that of power. The power oriented person will do well until someone steps on his power. Let anything cross him and he will be angry, sometimes unreasonably so. This is the person who wants others to jump when he says the word.

In one church a key lay leader, who always seemed to be a spiritual man and a generous giver to the Lord's work, left the church in anger. The pastor had not realized it, but the man had focused his anger on him. In their final discussion, the pastor attempted to help the situation by telling the man how sorry he was that he was leaving. With that the angry man said, "You remind me of my brother." Somehow, unresolved anger with his brother had been transferred to the pastor.

The candidate's attitude toward authority can measure his emotional stability. If a person has an authority problem, it usually is linked to his submission, or lack of it, to the Lord Jesus Christ. In law enforcement academies, candidates for police work are rejected if it is felt they have authority problems because they will lord it over the people they are supposed to serve. The same discernment should be operative in the church.

On the positive side, a spiritual leader should be able to handle authority because he is responsible for what he is assigned. He must be able to deal fairly and wisely with all but also be able to confront the rebellious if necessary. He should be able to accept criticism and be willing to improve himself for Christ's sake.

In the ministry of Christ, both lay leaders and professional leaders must be able to accept or endure criticism. They must be group builders, who give more than they get from their responsibility in leadership. They must be emotionally stable in order to carry the weight.

You will need to ask some closing questions about the subject of emotional stability. For instance, how does he treat his wife? Is he a bully in the home? How about his children? Does he relate to them with compassion and authority in balance? Or does he lose his temper and quench God's Spirit in his home? Is there a happy balance between husband and wife so that it is obvious he is the leader and she loves it?

Spiritual leaders need to be spiritually mature and emotionally prepared, for criticism is always leveled at them. Such criticism is one of the costs of leadership; it comes, as they say, with the territory. Criticism cannot be borne unless the qualities of spiritual and emotional maturity are part of the leader's life.

Remember that Elijah ran in fear just after he had defeated the prophets of Baal. Every spiritual leader suffers from the Elijah complex when the devil gets after him. There are times when all of us are tempted to turn and run. Spiritual maturity and emotional stability will help the spiritual leader say no to that temptation and remain steady on the job before the enemy's onslaughts.

4. Gifts and Abilities

The final important criterion for selecting a leadership candidate involves gifts and abilities. Putting valued spiritual gifts, skills, and abilities last does not take away from their importance. With motivation, godliness, and stability nailed down, we should now look for the best talent available.

When looking at a candidate for the pulpit, the gifts of preaching and teaching must be considered first. His skill as a student of the Bible and his natural ability as a communicator will also be important for his work as a preacher. All of the skills necessary for a successful ministry must be present.

The minister of music should, of course, be gifted musically. He must have a heart for worship and should be trained in the music field. His natural ability in singing, his personality, and other attributes also should be appreciated and valued.

In short, you will want to find the best skilled, gifted, and qualified person for the job, but only after the first three requirements have been met. The search for (1) motivation, (2) spiritual maturity, (3) emotional stability, and (4) gifts and abilities—in that order—has served me well for more than twenty-eight years in the pastorate.

These same criteria can be applied to any spiritual leadership role, lay or professional. They are valuable for Sunday school leaders, deacons, ministers, and virtually any potential leader.

Related Requisites for Effective Leaders

Starting with the more important ones, let us look to a secondary list of requirements for Christian leader effectiveness.

1. Faithfulness

The requirement of faithfulness is a must for the leadership recruit. To be faithful generally means to be a dedicated Christian who loves the Lord. The priorities of the Christian life are, for the faithful person, already settled: beliefs, lifestyle, and commitment to the life of the church.

But faithfulness in a leadership context also means an honest commitment on the part of the candidate to the leader who is to train him and to the training program itself. I have had to sit down with young men and women who want to intern with us and say, "Look, you do not want this badly enough. If you are unfaithful now, in training, so that you do not work at what you are given to do, what will you do later, when you are alone with no one to supervise you?" That is the dismissal speech. If they want to come back, they have to settle the question of faithfulness.

2. Availability

A leadership candidate must be available if he is to be trained. He must be willing to give his training a high priority and to set aside other things in order to accomplish it. This is a question of willingness to put first things first, and is also a question of whether the student can actually, physically be with you enough to fulfill his obligation.

In most cases, a motivated person will get where he needs to be. In Haiti I have seen Christians walk most of the night to be in church on Sunday. They wear their best clothes and sing all the way through six or seven miles of bush because they want to be at church. The candidate for leadership training must possess a similar willingness to make an all-out effort to be there.

3. Teachability

The candidate for leadership must be teachable. He must be eager to learn, willing to change, and have the capacity for intellectual and spiritual growth and development. With the other qualifications already mentioned, a person who is teachable at this point ought to have great potential for God's service. He will be worthy of the teacher's best efforts.

Proverbs 13:4 says, "The soul of a sluggard desires and has nothing; but the soul of the diligent shall be made rich." We pick up this idea and declare that the diligent is one who is Faithful, Available, and Teachable. Such a one has a "FAT," or rich, soul.

4. Self-motivation

Look for someone who gets going daily without having to be pushed. It is not important about what time a minister on staff gets into his office each day. What matters is that he has the initiative to make things happen without constant urging.

It is like the old story of the pastor who was asked why he went down to the crossing to watch the train come through every morning. He answered, "I just like to see something go that I don't have to energize." Spiritual leaders should not need to be pushed continually.

5. Industry

Find your leaders from among those who like to work. There are people who are so excited about Jesus Christ they love to work for Him.

People today do not readily learn how to work. Many have not learned how to give themselves to their work and expend their energy laboring. Industry suffers from laborers who think that if they just show up for work they have made their contributions for the day. That attitude must not carry over into the work of the kingdom.

6. Innovation

Spiritual leaders should not be content with the same old things that have never worked. The church is plagued with the we-have-always-done-it-this-way syndrome. The spiritual leader who can recognize and keep the ideas that work and discard the antiquated ones that no longer fly will be a great addition to the family of God.

7. Productivity

If your first staff member does not produce, you never will get a second one who does. That is because your congregation will not be willing to hire anyone else. In addition, a nonproducing staff member will discourage the senior pastor from calling others because of his poor showing. Sluggards slow everybody down.

8. Likemindedness

Those who work under an effective leader must hold to his philosophy of ministry. If the umbrella idea is going to work, the umbrella men are going to have to be of one mind.

The church I now serve was split over a difference in ministerial philosophy between the former pastor and a staff member. The men under the umbrella, ministers of various programs, must work in concert with their leader. A mark of the early church that accompanied their power was their unity and complete agreement about what they had to do. "Now when the Day of Pentecost had fully come, they were all with one accord in one place" (Acts 2:1).

I sometimes am asked by men and women who serve on other church staffs what they can do about getting the church into a program the pastor does not want. My answer is, "If the pastor won't go there, the church cannot." Disagreements can always be handled on minor points, but the general philosophy and direction should be agreed to unanimously by all in leadership. Spiritual leaders, working together, should be of one accord in their philosophy of ministry. That philosophy should be established by the pastor.

9. Interaction

The spiritual leaders you select must be able to work with the ministry team. Team players are not loners but mix well with other team members and contribute to the success of the whole. Some Christian leaders, for whatever reasons, like to work alone, as the only shepherd among the flock. I do not reprove what works for them, but umbrella men who want to see the church grow and see the borders of the kingdom of God expanded must work together. Teamwork is the very nature of the working of the body of Christ.

10. Seasoning

Ideally, the one you select for a leadership role should be nearing the height of his potential. Let him blossom out and reach his best performance while working with you. It is like picking a rose that is just breaking out of the bud and seeing it develop into a beautiful, full flower.

11. Stewardship

He must at least be a tither to the Lord's church. Although I have mentioned this earlier, it bears repeating: leaders should lead in their example of giving as in everything else.

12. Devotion

He must be strong in the Scriptures, both in convictions and practice. He must be a student of the Bible and read it devotionally as well. A spiritual leader must take his direction from the Word of God.

13. Camaraderie

Before having a new member come on staff, you should get to know him well enough to be able to answer all of the questions I have posed here. Familiarity with your candidate will eliminate a popular business method: acquiring a resumé on a prospective leader and selecting him on the basis of what is written about him rather than on the basis of personal knowledge. The resume is fine, but the candidate should be seen in his natural habitat. Otherwise, you might just be hiring a person who is gifted only at writing resumés! And he should get to know the umbrella man well enough to determine if he can work under his umbrella.

Who Chooses the Staff?

The question of who chooses the staff is crucial. The successes or failures of staff relationships depend on this decision.

There is no question in my mind that the pastor should select the church staff. His decision can be ratified by the board or congregation, but the pastor should seek and choose his own associates on the ministerial staff. The choosing must be done prayerfully, with the calling of God in mind. This is consistent with Moses' choosing seventy elders. God anointed them, but Moses chose them. The experience of Paul and Barnabas is also valid here. They chose their partners for their second journeys. Barnabas took John Mark, and Paul took Silas.

When An Associate Pastor Is Chosen

Great care should be taken by the pastor when he selects an associate. Too often pastors have called men to serve with them without asking for references from others who know the candidate well. I do not know whether this omission is done in ignorance or in the spirit of pirating someone from another staff. But I have seen much grief from such careless, impulsive moves on the part of senior pastors.

I have appreciated those pastors who have contacted me before they invite one of the men under my umbrella to come with them. This is both a courtesy and a means of inquiring about the candidate-in-question's present situation and profitability for the ministry.

I want to know a candidate for a staff position well. I want to hear from others who know him both as a minister and a family man. Time taken to work through these and other important considerations will pay off handsomely when you find the right person for the job.

The Care of Other Umbrella Men

Whether or not the church can grow and reach its potential will depend on how the pastor, who holds the big umbrella, cares for those who serve with him and how much he will let them serve. The spiritual leaders who lead and develop the smaller umbrellas are also umbrella men and, as such, are anointed by God for their ministries. They lead the ministries in youth programs, Christian education, lay evangelism, discipleship groups, and other works. But both the size and effectiveness of their ministries will depend first of all on the pastor, who inspires them with oversight, support, protection, and spiritual nurture.

The first thing a pastor has to do to become a true umbrella man is to stop thinking of the church as "my ministry." If care is not taken, soon he will think "my pulpit" and "my staff" and "my church."

Here is a good place to start: simply drop the word *my* from your vocabulary. Our words say more sometimes than we intend for them to say. If we say "my ministry" and mean our part in the ministry, that is one thing, but ownership must belong to God. If we really accept that, we can serve boldly and effectively, and at the same time get ourselves out of the way.

One young associate pastor was frustrated because the senior pastor he worked under would not allow him to work very much with the people. The senior pastor seemed afraid to let go of anything of importance. Even visitation of the sick in hospitals was off limits unless the senior pastor had already made an initial call on the patient. The young associate was not allowed to do as much as trained laymen do in some churches. Yet, he was exceptionally capable. Since then he has gone on to become a very effective preacher and pastor in another church. The practice of muzzling God's servants and restricting their service and contribution to the Lord's church is a serious one and must be handled. Spiritual leaders need to open things up and get away from defensiveness.

A Model Leader

Any discussion of leading a multiple pastoral staff has to begin with Moses and his struggles in the desert with a cantankerous and complaining congregation. If ever a man had too much to carry on his shoulders, it was Moses. He said to the Lord every day what most of us in leadership say on Monday, "Why have You afflicted Your servant? And why have I not found favor in Your sight, that You have laid the burden of all these people on me?" (Num. 11:11).

Like so many pastors, Moses was tired, ragged, and all but burned out with so many challenges and too much to do. Moses had about had it! He came very near to insubordination when he spoke to God as he did, but

God understood and had a solution all ready for him. Moses needed help.

The Lord's solution was for Moses to select seventy elders of Israel to serve with him. Help at last! God said to him, "Then I will come down and talk with you there. I will take of the Spirit that is upon you, and will put the same upon them; and they shall bear the burden of the people with you that you may not bear it yourself alone" (Num. 11:17). Moses recruited them; God appointed them as Moses' assistants, and then God anointed them. Then they had a ministry team. That is the way a staff should be called. The pastor selects them; God appoints them through the governing body, and God anoints them. Moses was the first umbrella man and he showed us how to be one.

Right away something happened that today often upsets pastors and destroys pastoral staffs: when God anointed the elders, they prophesied. That is, they spoke a message from God. "And the Spirit rested upon them. Now they were among those listed, but who had not gone out to the tabernacle; yet they prophesied in the camp" (Num. 11:26). In turn, each man prophesied and then stopped speaking—except for two men, Eldad and Medad. They went out among the people preaching!

A young man ran to tell Moses about it. It was Joshua. Afraid that Moses' authority was being threatened, Joshua urged Moses to stop them from speaking. How often we do the same thing! We fail when we fear for ourselves and our status and impose ourselves between God and His purpose. Moses refused Joshua's request.

This is not a discussion, by the way, about the "plurality of elders" concept where everyone has equal authority, as some of my colleagues say. I know that Jesus said in Matthew 23:8, "One is your Teacher, the Christ, and you are all brethen." We are all equal, true. However, some bear more responsibility than others; that is to say, some are first among equals. It is not a question of equality, but of whom God is holding responsible. That is not an honor per se; it is an assignment. In fact, Moses called it a burden.

Moses was clearly the man in charge, with responsibility from God to lead the people. One cannot overlook that point in Scripture. And the thing that made Moses shine was his attitude. He was not proud; he was tired and knew he needed help.

Moses' answer to Joshua's objection was his greatest statement on leadership. He voiced an attitude that should be heard everywhere in Christian circles today. Moses said, "Are you zealous for my sake? Oh, that all the LORD's people were prophets and that the LORD would put His Spirit upon them!" (Num. 11:29). God's man knew his calling and was not afraid of the spiritual power and gifts for others called to serve under him. His own inability to grapple with his task, without their help, was well-known to him. Instead of being immobilized by the frustration of it all, he could get on with his mission. Moses could care for all the people with the help of the seventy elders.

Three Elements in Ongoing Leadership

A major goal of each church staff should be to enjoy longevity together with a minimum turnover. To do that, they need to consider what makes a staff member happy and productive in his or her work. The worker, I believe, needs three basic underpinnings in his ministry to make him both a motivated team member and a producer.

1. Worth: A worker needs to know his task is worth doing. Then he receives a sense of self-worth from his job. The value of his work is of primary importance.

Once I labored in an aircraft factory where an assembler could work all day on one part, only to have the inspector come by and stamp it NG for "no good." The entire day's work would go into the trash bin. Often the worker would go home frustrated. With a little supervision and guidance, he could have done his work correctly the first time. Today, things are changing. American industrialists have learned to bring their employees together to show them why their individual tasks are worthy and crucial to the whole.

A retired air force colonel became a Christian and was excited about his new life in Christ. But when he joined the church, his joy was short-lived. Instead of being nurtured and brought along as a new Christian, he was assigned busywork as the assistant chairman of a nonessential committee. Soon the colonel dropped out of the church. Let church leaders learn that busywork and the drudgery of committee meetings eliminate more Christian workers than Satan's best efforts.

In the colonel's case the Christian faith was made to seem unworthy through unworthy tasks. If he had been given an opportunity to serve in a spiritual ministry as a disciple, he would have felt the supreme worthiness of Christ's work and gone on to bigger assignments. Fortunately, he joined another congregation and is serving with them today.

The remedy? Cut out busywork altogether. Concentrate on the really important needs facing people today. Prayer is the most needed ministry in the church. Everywhere in the world where the Lord is blessing there are God's people praying. Instead of organizing committees that never seem to work, let God's people gather into prayer groups to pray to Him. Form home Bible study groups and neighborhood evangelistic Bible studies for prayer and the ministry of God's Word.

The sense of worthiness in the work of Christ must begin with spiritual leaders. Those who value the ministry will make it important and cause others to see it that way, too. An umbrella man has to be so committed and excited about his work that he draws others under the umbrella and motivates them to give their all for the Lord.

I marvel at the way football coaches motivate their players to knock people down and kick the football between the uprights. A while back, I preached to an NFL team at its chapel meeting before a game. I watched the coach's incredible ability as a motivator. When he talked to me for a moment about my work in Modesto, he was interested in what I was doing. The coach convinced me I had to make a *winner* out of the church, not just an also-ran. His voice began to rise, and I felt myself being caught up in his enthusiasm.

Later, I thought how much we pastors lack in visible motivation for the Lord's work. The coach made football seem the most worthwhile thing in the world. And when he talked to me, he made the church seem so important I could not fail to make a renewed all-out effort to win for the Lord.

The umbrella man's work is cut out for him; the Lord's work will be as worthy and as important to the people as *he* thinks it is.

2. *Dignity:* No matter how big or small the task, whether paid or voluntary, there must be dignity in

doing it. When workers are shown respect and are honored as people, as well as for the tasks they are doing, they will walk with dignity and be happy to serve.

Status brings dignity. This is well-known in industries where job titles have been changed to bring dignity to the tasks. Janitors first were upgraded to custodians, and then sanitation engineers. Tractor drivers are no longer cat skinners, but heavy equipment operators. Housewives are called homemakers. But the name of the task is not nearly so important as the way the person doing it is treated. Whatever his title, each person has a dignity all his own as a child of God.

Whether a man works in a sewer, handling the filth of the city, or in the antiseptically clean operating room of a hospital, he should be honored with dignity as a person. The attitude of a spiritual leader will come through no matter what his work is. The wise spiritual leader will regard every person with dignity, regardless of his occupation.

When I was in high school, a friend came to my home one evening crying bitter tears. His father had just been killed in an auto accident. Grief was added to grief because the family had always looked down on him as a common laborer. They saw, too late, that they had looked at the job and missed the person. Christian leaders must know there is great dignity in the one who chooses to serve God in even the most menial task. "For a day in Your courts is better than a thousand. I would rather be a doorkeeper in the house of my God than dwell in the tents of wickedness" (Ps. 84:10).

3. Recognition: A word of appreciation and recognition for work done is like a breath of life to some. One of our young interns told about the joy and motivation he felt when the pastor who was his training supervisor put his arm around him one day and said, "Sam, you are really doing some good work. We all love you around here, brother. You are going to make it in the ministry." This gesture was especially important to Sam because no one in his family showed outward affection or approval. It was the first time in his life that anyone had said something like that to him. We are instructed to "be kindly affectionate to one another with brotherly love, in honor giving preference to one another" (Rom. 12:10).

A review of a worker's productivity and accomplishments—or even his failures—is a kind of recognition. I have met with dozens of associate pastors, youth workers, and Christian education men who were frustrated because they did not really know how they were doing. One said to me, "We never meet to go over what I am doing so I don't really know if I'm making it or not. At this point, even a rebuke would be welcome."

Many pastors who love the Lord and preach well are poor umbrella men when it comes to caring for those under their umbrellas. Praise for work well done and correction in the right spirit for work not well done are both forms of badly needed recognition.

Recognition and appreciation can be shown in other ways: kind words, public praise, prayers of thanks, rewards of time off, and material gifts. Some of the least appreciated workers in the church are the nursery aides, children's workers, ushers, and people who help as greeters or assist with the parking. Pastors and those who are before the congregation tend to receive recognition and praise (along with complaints) from church members; others are not recognized for their labors at all. Here is a need the umbrella man can care for. Recognition of work well done, along with sincere expressions of appreciation, will help and encourage those who labor long and hard under the big umbrella.

Ye Olde Bottom Line

Too often in the church we see under the umbrella man associate ministers who give almost every waking hour to the ministry but receive too little compensation. They sacrifice and struggle to serve the Lord, while their families are neglected.

Recognition of ministers and their families through adequate salary and expenses should be standard procedure. In 1 Timothy 5:17 we are instructed to care for the elders. "Let the elders who rule well be counted worthy of double honor, especially those who labor in the word and doctrine." The next verse seems to indicate that "double honor" means double compensation: "'You shall not muzzle an ox while it treads out the grain', and, 'the laborer is worthy of his wages'" (1 Tim. 5:18).

A good umbrella man ought to care for the men under him out of concern for their families and their needs. I have never had to ask the board or the church for anything for myself, but I often have spoken for the other staff. Failure to compensate these men and women of God according to the Scripture is not only failure to obey God, it is not good business for the church. It often happens that a skilled and dedicated minister will give himself to his work for a time but then be called away to a church which recognizes his worth and offers him a commensurate salary. He cannot be blamed for leaving if his welfare has been ignored.

When a minister does have to leave in order to care for his family, the church not only loses his services and the benefit of all that he has learned on the job, it loses money too. If a man is underpaid and doing a good job, his replacement cost will be far more than the additional salary he could be given to meet his needs. In addition, the church loses all of the relationships the man has developed. The effect of losing people who drop by the wayside is incalculable.

I once heard a pastor say, "I want to find someone who is so dedicated he will work cheap." That kind of attitude is unworthy of a spiritual leader. My answer to that is, let the undedicated fellow work cheap. The umbrella man must see to it that those who work under his care receive enough to live on. God will honor a spiritual leader for such caring concern.

Care by Communicating

Communication is an absolute necessity for staff relationships. It must begin with the pastor and invite response throughout the staff. It is difficult for staff members to initiate conversations with a nonspeaking, noncommunicating leader. (Take care that the quiet qualities of leadership not be *too* quiet.)

Communication should begin the new man's first day on the job. A welcome from the leader and the assurance that the new person is needed and wanted on the team is invaluable. I can still remember the first person who welcomed me aboard when I got my first fulltime job. His consideration for my nervousness and sense of being a stranger in a place where everyone else knew one another made him my friend automatically.

Communication should continue through informal conversations, planned meetings, and social times. The pastor himself does not want to be treated like the hired gun, the special agent who must do all of the spiritual tracking, with no concern shown for him personally. Likewise he should not treat the staff as hit men for Jesus who work for money and serve without recognition.

Regular staff meetings are essential. I have always held regular weekly staff meetings on Wednesday mornings. We begin at 8:30 and finish at noon, with lunch together for the whole staff once each month. Our meetings include Bible sharing, prayer, and an agenda.

Three times each year the staff gets away for three-day planning meetings. We call them "staff attacks" rather than retreats. Our attitude is that we are going to move things forward. It is important to spend time together as a staff and to play together as well as work hard together. Communication must also involve communion and sharing as a community. It is being part of a family together, loving one another.

Care by Protecting

The church staff, as with other umbrella men, are vulnerable and need protection. This is where the idea of the umbrella is most viable. Not only is there need for a wholesome, friendly, spiritual environment, but there is need for protection under the umbrella. The staff member who knows the leader will back him up in a tight place will be motivated to go all out in his efforts. If he is unsupported when he is contradicted, falsely accused, or slandered, the wind will go out of his sails and he will cease to be effective.

Protection also should include looking after matters of health, fatigue, and other physical needs. Many times men on the staff have begun to look haggard and worn.

If you look closely you can see signs of fatigue or sickness in a man's eyes. I have made it a practice to provide time off and to offer assistance to those on the staff who seem to be hurting in this way. Sometimes they need protection from overburdened schedules and from pressures at home that can be helped by a caring word or deed from the one they regard as their spiritual leader.

Care of the Staff's Children

I have a tender spot in my heart for "preachers' kids." Being raised in a minister's home should provide benefits for a child. He should be happy to have his father be a minister of the gospel, but certain things are necessary. The minister must have adequate compensation, as I have already said, and he must have time off to be with his family. Use of the term *quality time* can be an excuse for short vacations. It is good if the time a pastor spends with his family has quality, but he needs a *quantity* of time to make all that quality worthwhile!

A full day off during the week and *at least* one other night each week at home with the family is essential for health. When our children were young we set aside Friday evening as family night. We usually stayed at home. If the umbrella man encourages this kind of family togetherness, other umbrella men are more likely to take time for their families.

To Whom Does a Pastor Talk?

One great benefit of having an umbrella ministry is the mutual support the staff lends to one another. I often am asked, "Whom do you go to when you have a problem and need someone to talk to?" Other than Barbara, I can talk to my friend on staff, Loyal Friesen, or my preaching partner, Ron Blanc, or any of the others on the team. They benefit from the same kind of help and friendship from me and from one another, as do their wives.

Their children also have other pastors to talk to, other than their dads, if they feel the need for privacy. Then there is prayer, offered by the whole staff, when one is in need. Under the big umbrella is a wonderful place to raise a family.

Finally, there are fellow pastors in other churches. *Leadership* magazine carried the story of a Nazarene pastor who had as his spiritual guide an Episcopal priest. Both men were committed to the lordship of Christ, and the friendship that developed between them was of great value to both.

Courage to Confront

Let us understand that when there are problems we are to confront them in order to help the people who are involved. These people should not be regarded as problem people. They need help from others in the body of Christ.

Gordon MacDonald once asked me what it takes to be a good confronter. My answer was that he should not enjoy doing it. Confrontation must be seen as a spiritual undertaking—a ministry given. It is never easy to do.

Confrontation should not be combative. It should not be done in a belligerent way, but it should be conciliatory and helpful. Neither should it be carried out only as a last resort. Confrontation is intended by God to keep the body of Christ healthy. It is to be therapeutic, healing misunderstandings and clearing away sin. It is to keep the body of Christ clean from error, bitterness, and ungodly behavior. It is a way God has given us to help members of the church learn by their mistakes and grow in the process.

A Typical Problem

One Sunday Dave came home from church in a miserable state of mind. He was fuming about the acquisition of two lots adjacent to the church property. His pastor had made the announcement in the morning service.

Although he was a member of the board, Dave had not objected to the proposal when it was discussed in the meeting earlier in the month because he did not want to be the only one to object. But, after the meeting, he had approached the other board members to complain as they headed for their cars. Then in the final meeting, when the vote was taken, he had said nothing. Dave became angry with himself for not having enough courage to confront the issue when he should have.

At home with his wife, Florence, and their nine-year-old son, Dan, Dave started grumbling. He complained about the unnecessary expense of the land purchase. He called the board members "yes men" and bitterly denounced the pastor as a dictator who would lead the church to ruin. The other family members listened in silence, but soon the seeds of bitterness found a foothold. Florence and Dan became angry, too.

That night, Dave and his family did not go to church. On Wednesday, he resigned from the choir. The following day he wrote a letter to the pastor, resigning from the board. Dave continued to pronounce his judgment upon the pastor and church leaders. Florence began reflecting her husband's critical spirit, complaining to the other women of the church.

Young Dan loved his father very much. He figured that the pastor and the people down at the church were hurting his daddy, so he began to act out his bitterness. As he grew older, he became disruptive in church services.

After a time, Dave repented of his attitude and soon was back singing in the choir. But still angry, Dan resented his father for changing his mind. Years passed. As he grew older, Dan was on the outside edge of things. He never got involved, and his father's urgings about going to youth meetings at church only made him more rebellious.

When a new youth director came, Dave urged his son to get involved. But Dan continued to be disruptive at the meetings—or absent altogether. Finally, when his father pressured him, Dan had an answer. "Fine youth pastor he is!" he countered. "He isn't even teaching the Bible!" He knew that objection would score big with his dad.

Right on cue, Dave went straight to the pastor. "Do you know that youth director of yours is not teaching the Bible, and my son has had it with the group?" he charged.

The pastor was intimidated and the umbrella was nowhere in sight. He did not back up his man. Instead, he was stunned by the accusation and reacted by calling in the youth minister and demanding, "Why haven't you been teaching the Bible to these kids?" The youth pastor stood in silence while the pastor lectured him about the church's commitment to Scripture.

The failure to confront the real problem brought down, in shreds, what little was left of the spiritual umbrella. Soon after, the youth pastor left the ministry. It was the second time he had been undercut in his brief career. But things went on as usual at the church. The pastor called another youth director. Dave went on singing in the choir. Florence gradually dropped out of committees. And Dan left home and joined the Marines.

What Should Have Been Done?

What went wrong in the church and with Dave's family? What could have been done to prevent it?

The problem goes back to the original board meeting where the proposal was discussed. Dave should have been asked to speak up. If he had refused, he should have been encouraged privately to tell what was troubling him. The pastor and board chairman did not hear the thundering silence in Dave. And, when he went to others after the meeting to complain, someone on the board should have confronted him with his bad attitude. The choir director did not follow through either when Dave abruptly resigned. Because the choir director was not involved in the dispute, he could have been helpful to his longtime friend.

The root of bitterness, when planted and nourished, can grow into a large, cancerous organism. The Bible warns us to beware of it, "looking diligently lest anyone fall short of the grace of God; lest any root of bitterness springing up cause trouble, and by this many become defiled" (Heb. 12:15).

A caring church would have reached out to Dave, had it known of his plight. This is where the ministry of confrontation can have such a therapeutic effect. So many times former church members blaspheme the church and its Lord because of the root of bitterness that might have been healed if confrontation had been administered in the right way. Church splits and even broken homes begin with this kind of bitterness. I have seen individuals, and then families, and then whole Sunday school classes come snarling into church business meetings, spoiling for a fight because the bitterness was not snipped off before it took root.

If the pastor did not know of Dave's efforts to circumvent their decision, he certainly knew something was wrong when Dave resigned from the board. A consultation with Dave, with prayer and words of encouragement and exhortation at the right moment, might have saved the church and Dave's family from the hurts that were to come as a result of his bitterness. It is always better to solve a problem while it is being kindled, like a little campfire, before it gets out of control than to wait until it flares up, like a raging brushfire.

Had Dave been offered an opportunity to ventilate his feelings to a pastor willing to listen to opposition, he might have been won over. Some people need more care than others. It is wise to discover which ones need ventilating.

I once knew a man who needed to get things off his chest about every six weeks. He was a good man, but he was bothered because he would almost never speak up and find out what he needed to know. Or he would disagree with a group decision and keep it to himself. He understood, finally, that I knew his problem and tried to help by periodically letting him ventilate. After that, he called me "wise guy" whenever he saw me. It was meant as a compliment.

The Shepherd's Rod

Another time, a church was destroyed because its pastor could not bring himself to confront an attack on himself and the congregation. He was a shepherd who could not use the rod of confrontation.

A pastor sometimes makes the mistake of allowing the one he counsels to tell too much about himself. Then every time the counselee sees the pastor, he imagines a threat: the pastor knows too much, even though he keeps confidence.

This was the situation with a deacon's wife who became angry with her pastor and poured out her anger on her husband. What happened next only occurs in nightmares for most pastors.

The woman's husband had been a leading deacon in the church. As he heard his wife's accusations against the pastor, he grew angry and expressed his bitterness to the other board members. The complaint involved mostly petty matters, like criticism of the pastor's clothing and displeasure with his salary. But questions also were raised about his preaching and even his call to the ministry.

Finally, six deacons and their wives decided to take the situation into their own hands and confront the pastor during the evening worship service. Word was sent to him that the group would be present on Sunday night.

The worried pastor called me on Saturday to ask for prayer and counsel. We prayed. Then I advised him to get to the objectors that very afternoon and speak to them face to face in the hope of resolving the conflict before the church was destroyed. I read 2 Timothy 2:24–25: "And a servant of the Lord must not quarrel but be gentle to all, able to teach, patient, in humility correcting those who are in opposition, if God perhaps will grant them repentance, so that they may know the truth."

People who picture the shepherd as a leaf trembling in the wind should know that a shepherd of old carried a rod and a staff for the protection of his sheep. The trouble today is that few people actually understand the shepherd's role. The shepherd today must carry the rod of confrontation. He must work to reconcile differences, but when he encounters those who are out to destroy the church, he must follow Paul's instruction in Titus 1:10–11 which says, "For there are many insubordinate, both idle talkers and deceivers, especially those of the circumcision, whose mouths must be stopped." Paul goes on to tell Titus to "rebuke them sharply" (v. 13).

I once had to deal with a similar group of sheep rustlers in the church. A man and his wife were intent on creating a power group to turn the church back to its old ineffective ways. Their plan was to gather new believers into their fold, essentially to poison them against me. They even took training for prayer room counseling so they could get the new lambs right out of the prayer room. Then, they would invite them to their home to turn them away from my leadership and enlist them in their sheep-stealer's conspiracy.

When I found out what was happening, I told them to their faces that if they responded to the invitation to counsel anymore, I would stop them before the entire congregation and expose them for what they were. There was nothing conciliatory to be done at this point. They had to be stopped. And that did it!

Unhappily, the pastor threatened by the belligerent group did nothing. He spent a sleepless night and then somehow made it through a sermon on Sunday morning. Then on Sunday night it happened!

Partway into the evening service, as a hymn was being sung, they came in. All six deacons stood in the middle aisle of the church facing the pastor, squarely in front of the pulpit, their wives crowding the aisle with them. Without explanation, they read what by now had become a tirade against the man of God and his wife.

Shaken, the pastor stood passively as they completed their ungodly mission and stormed out the door. Everyone listened as they drove their cars out of the church parking lot, wheels screeching. Then, without trying to finish the sermon, the pastor dismissed the people and went home to agonize with his wife and family.

The pastor left almost immediately to take another church. But the little congregation, crippled by the destructive loss of its leadership, soon gave up. The church was disbanded and its property sold. A shopping mall now stands where a church once upheld the Word of God.

The church was destroyed because the courage to confront was missing in the pastor who was responsible for the care of the flock. Umbrella men will know how to meet aggression and how to deal with such aggressors through confrontation. That is the idea of the umbrella: it protects. But it requires *courage*, brother shepherds, to be an umbrella man.

Where no leadership exists, other leaders will arise.

When a Brother Needs Help

Christians are instructed to restore someone who is caught in a trespass. We are told in Galatians 6:1 how that man is to be treated: "Brethren, if a man is overtaken in any trespass, you who are spiritual restore such a one in a spirit of gentleness, considering yourself lest you also be tempted."

It is said that the Christian army is the only army in the world that buries its wounded alive. It is true that in many places those who are caught in really notable sins are condemned. But it is also true that often such fallen comrades are ignored and allowed to drift away, lost in their sins.

Believers are instructed to restore the brother, neither ignoring him nor pouncing upon him to cast him out. The word *restore* here means to help the brother correct his way with confession and repentance, to establish him again to where he was before. The ones to do the restoring are those who walk in the Spirit. A mark of their spirituality is to be found in the way they seek to restore their fallen brother.

Who are the spiritual ones? They are the ones Jesus spoke about in Matthew 7:1–5 who have repented and have cleansed their lives. The instruction begins with "Judge not, that you be not judged" and ends with "Hypocrite! First remove the plank from your own eye, and then you will see clearly to remove the speck out of your brother's eye." While the first importance of the lesson Jesus taught is a warning against judging, He does not eliminate confronting a brother to help him.

Without true humility, a would-be confronter is no more than a busybody. Such people cause much harm and have no place in this discussion. Confrontation to restore a fallen brother is only for those who walk with God. And godly help that comes from a spiritual believer can be administered to a brother in a spirit of gentleness, which is a fruit of the Spirit.

A woman in the church was a terrible gossip. She used her telephone to broadcast her latest information on this person and that person. Her compulsion to talk monopolized other people's time through most of the waking hours. Because of her gossip, the church was hurting. Something had to be done.

Then two women in leadership went to the gossiper

and confronted her with the problem as gently as possible. They offered their help. First they began to meet with the woman every week for prayer and Bible study. Soon the woman was involved in a Bible study group and began to feel accountable to the group for her actions. Then she was invited to become involved in evangelism training where she began to blossom and grow. Gossiping stopped entirely for her. She became a witness for Christ.

Later, she gave this testimony in the church: "I like to talk. But I had nothing to talk about before, so I talked about people. Now I can talk about Jesus Christ, and I want to thank those who helped me to find myself so I can witness for my Lord."

If help can be given so easily, then what is it that keeps Christians from restoring their brothers and sisters? The fear of judging, ignorance of the Word, and an unwillingness to get involved seem to be the stumbling blocks that keep the church from utilizing confrontation. There are also those who find it easier to judge than to assist. But confrontation in the way of restoration is a healing balm that is much needed in the church today.

We are living in a time like Jesus' day, when even God's people are willing to see a brother wounded and bleeding and walk around him, while all the time the Lord is looking for a good Samaritan. Perhaps confrontation needs not so much courage, but a heart that is right with God.

Self-confrontation and getting the planks out of our own eyes have to come first. Along with this cleansing, however, is the need to have the right attitude. There are two verses that have helped me immensely in approaching a person caught in a trespass.

James 1:20 reads, "For the wrath of man does not produce the righteousness of God." No matter how much I may be disturbed by what I see and hear, I am instructed to "be swift to hear, slow to speak, slow to wrath." (James 1:19). Even though the quiet quality of being slow to anger is sometimes hard to find, persist and keep your heart guarded from the temptation to lose your temper.

The second thought comes from Proverbs 15:1, "A soft answer turns away wrath, but a harsh word stirs up anger." During confrontation, the attitude of a godly man will show. If he wants to help his brother, the spirit of gentleness will be his way of approaching the brother in need. The responsibility of restoring a trespassing brother is never intended to prompt a witch hunt. It is to unite the body of Christ when one member is hurting and in danger and another is able to help.

Help! Someone Sinned against Me!

How do we behave when someone sins against us? Too often we start a counteroffensive, and the war begins. That is the human way, and it is wrong.

The teaching of our Lord is very clear. "Moreover if your brother sins against you, go and tell him his fault between you and him alone. If he hears you, you have gained your brother. But if he will not hear you, take with you one or two more, that 'by the mouth of two or three witnesses every word may be established.' And if he refuses to hear them, tell it to the church. But if he refuses even to hear the church, let him be to you like a heathen and a tax collector" (Matt. 18:15–17).

The question arises, "What does it mean to tell it to the church?" I seriously doubt the Lord had in view here every last man, woman, and child on the roll. I have applied "tell it to the church" to informing the official board of the church rather than standing before the congregation en masse and embarrassing the innocent ones in the family. This is especially important in light of court cases involving elders who have been brought to trial and convicted of slandering church members. If the sinner refuses to listen and repent of the sin and rejects the evidence of witnesses, he must be expelled. Remember, the sin here is something *serious*.

The words "if your brother sins" are understood to mean sin against another person, an act committed to bring loss or harm, not merely a failing in someone's character. It must be a willful sin committed against someone. If more than one person is sinned against, then all injured parties are to confront the offender.

A young pastor, just beginning in his first church, ran into a problem that demanded confrontation. A leading member of the board of deacons explained to him that he could not give to the church because he had committed his whole tithe to supporting a lifelong friend who was then a missionary to India. In his inexperience, the young pastor agreed that mission work was important and it was acceptable if the deacon did not tithe through the church.

Today the pastor says he would not make that mistake again. If faced with the same decision, he would insist that leaders lead—and that includes giving to the church. To help the deacon, he would have him give through the church and have the church support the missionary.

Why was the decision wrong? A few years later, the missionary came home on furlough and the pastor met him for the first time. He was a fine man of God. Trying to be supportive, the pastor told the missionary he was glad their mutual friend's tithe went to support his work. In amazement, the missionary said, "His tithe didn't come to me! In fact, he told me he could not give to missions because he was committed to the local church."

They had an Ananias on their hands! Together, they read the account of Peter's confrontation with Ananias very carefully and prayed together. Then the missionary and the pastor together confronted their brother.

The guidelines laid down by Jesus in Matthew 18: 15–17 are helpful and clear. First, take note that the offender is a brother. Next, be sure of the facts of the sin. Then, go to him privately. That means in a place where both can talk. Privacy protects all parties.

At the meeting, reprove or convict him by showing him the evidence. That will make it clear that he is guilty and the time has come for repentance and, if warranted, restitution. If done in the right spirit, this kind of confrontation (which nobody likes) can have a happy result. Wrongs can be righted, friendships restored, and the body of Christ healed.

The deacon in this case was overwhelmed with guilt and immediately repented. When he saw his pastor with his missionary friend, the deacon knew he had been exposed. At the time of the confrontation the pastor had shown him the danger of lying about his giving. His sin was not in failing to give, but in lying. He read the words of Peter, especially in Acts 5:4, "'While it remained, was it not your own? And after it was sold, was it not in your own control? Why have you conceived this thing in your heart? You have not lied to men but to God.'" For the first time the deacon saw the immensity of his sin and begged forgiveness, which was gladly granted. His confronters then prayed with the erring deacon and asked God to forgive and restore him.

It may take more than one session before hope is exhausted in the privacy stage and the next step must be taken. However, if the brother refuses to listen, we are to obey and take two or more witnesses to establish the facts. All of these efforts are to be aimed at restoring the brother.

Tell It to the Church

When the one who has sinned refuses to listen to witnesses and rejects all promptings of repentance and reconciliation, the facts must be told to the church. I mentioned earlier that I hesitate to broadcast a serious sin to the entire congregation. Let me elaborate on that conviction.

In the time when the Scripture was written, the church was led solely by men; women were not involved in a leadership capacity. This is still true in the orthodox Jewish synagogues. Telling sin to the church meant telling it to the men of the church. Today, that would mean telling the sin to a business session of the official board, which represents the whole. This will protect other church members from gory details or a burden they do not need to bear. Furthermore, there would be horrible embarrassment to a family whose husband and father falls into sin and will not repent.

In my experience, I have found that sexual sin is usually the only sin that will blind a person so completely that he or she will not repent. I will give an example in a moment. In most other cases repentance will come by means of confrontation. The warning to beware lest the confronter become caught up in the same sin that has captured his brother is, I think, a warning against sexual sins.

The final step is harsh but necessary. Failing all else, the unrepentant offender is to be expelled from the church. He is to be treated as a Gentile, or one who is outside the fold. He is to be regarded as a tax-gatherer, or one who has separated himself from Israel. The former member has really cast himself out from the body of Christ by his failure to repent.

Where There Is Immorality

Sexual immorality in the church must always be dealt with swiftly. Every minister and spiritual leader should keep himself reminded of the powerful effect this sin has upon the individual and upon the church. We are instructed in 1 Corinthians 6:18 to "flee sexual immorality. Every sin that a man does is outside the body, but he who commits sexual immorality sins against his own body." This is not a sin to pamper or try to overcome. It overpowers, conquers, and destroys.

The remedy is to flee, to keep away from the temptation. The flight has to begin with self-discipline in controlling what the mind and spirit feed upon. It has to mean breaking old patterns and establishing a spiritual walk. Sadly, some servants of God have had formal training and are marvelously equipped technicians but have never developed their own spiritual walks, with disciplines of holiness. These servants are very susceptible to the immorality that has inundated the church.

Now this question: what does the umbrella man do when an under umbrella man is found to be involved in sexual immorality? His first concern must be to protect the church. There must be no attempt to sweep the sin under the rug.

When cover-ups occur, the entire church suffers. At Corinth, Paul reprimanded the church for allowing such sins. They apparently were proud of what was happening. He said, "Your glorying is not good. Do you not know that a little leaven leavens the whole lump?" (1 Cor. 5:6). Leavening of the whole lump means that if the problem goes unchecked it will spread to the entire church. When leaders are caught up in this sin, they no longer can see clearly to stamp out the infection.

Therefore, the course of action for the umbrella man is clear. When immorality is found to be in the church, especially in leadership, he must act quickly. And he must follow the instructions in Scripture.

However, great care must be taken to ensure that no one is falsely accused or unfairly judged. I am very concerned with helping staff members—under umbrella men—when they face accusations. God's warning in Psalm 105:15 to the kings of old, concerning His servants, has impressed me deeply. "'Do not touch My anointed ones, and do My prophets no harm.'" Every umbrella man should have that Scripture hidden in his heart. Remember that anyone can be accused of wrongdoing. We are instructed to refuse an accusation against an elder unless there are two or three witnesses to prove the charge.

Remember too that every child of God is His anointed one today. Therefore, special care must be taken with every believer to protect his or her reputation. As an umbrella man, I want to be very sure to serve and protect the church as God's shepherd, but I must be very careful to follow God's instructions in order to protect His leaders.

How One Church Dealt with a Tough Problem

An associate minister on a certain church staff admittedly was involved in adultery. Here are the steps that were taken.

Galatians 6:1 had to be applied quickly. "Brethren, if a man is overtaken in any trespass, you who are spiritual restore such a one in a spirit of gentleness, considering yourself lest you also be tempted."

The pastor, within minutes after getting the facts, took another member of the pastoral staff to confront their brother, in the hope of restoring him. The man openly admitted his guilt but refused to repent. At this point the sin was not known in the church, except to the pastor and one staff member.

When the offender refused to repent, two more members of the staff were called in to pray and attempt to persuade the man to repent. Again he refused. That afternoon, the entire pastoral staff was assembled in an attempt to influence the man to repent. Again he refused. All was done that could be done to restore him. The next painful steps had to be taken.

God is clear in His instructions to His church in this matter. (1) "Do not receive an accusation against an elder except from two or three witnesses" (1 Timothy 5:19). (2) "Those who are sinning rebuke in the presence of all, that the rest also may fear" (1 Timothy 5:20). I have included verse 19 here to remind us that in a case like this there must be absolutely no doubt about the offender's guilt. Verse 20 leaves no doubt either about the seriousness of the sin and how the offender must be exposed if he will not repent. These verses should be read

118

to him so he will know what is coming if he refuses to repent and insists upon his sinful way.

All that has been related thus far happened in one day. In the initial stage, the problem had been contained within the church staff. Then the board of deacons had to be informed. The scriptural procedures that were followed by the pastor and staff were explained and the deacons expressed their sorrow and their agreement that the pastor should move quickly to inform the church.

That was done verbally and by letter to the congregation. The letter was sent to explain the procedures followed and the effort made to restore the man. The emphasis was on the attempt to restore, rather than on the man's sin.

The letter sent shock waves through the congregation, but they received it well, knowing that all was done that could have been done to restore the man. The pastor and members of the staff spoke personally to those lay people who had worked with the man, in order to reassure them that nothing more could have been done to help him before the final action was taken.

Why was a letter sent? In the case of a lay person so involved, the procedure would have been to tell it to the official board as I noted earlier. But in the case of a minister, more detail has to be given. Other means of communication may be used, but God's people must be completely informed. Otherwise, some might think a man of God is being falsely accused.

The leaders must have their facts correct, and they must be careful to follow prayerfully the instructions in the Word of God, especially Deuteronomy 19:15 which says, "One witness shall not rise against a man concerning any iniquity or any sin that he commits; by the mouth of two or three witnesses the matter shall be established."

That kind of confrontation requires immense courage. However, without it, the church will be weak and often ruled by sinners who will bring it to defeat. Confrontation is a means by which sin is kept out of the camp. Such is the work of umbrella men who, like leaders of old, are responsible for the well-being of the flocks of God under their umbrellas.

Four Crucial Steps in Leading by Example

Dr. Milton David is an orthopedic surgeon and chairman of our board of deacons. He is convinced that leading by example is the most effective way a spiritual leader can inspire others. He really has learned that leaders *lead*.

The church leadership was to be involved in making prayer visits throughout the membership. The deacons and staff were to lead the way and encourage others to follow. Dr. David and his wife, Carol, were successful in making all but one visit. They just could not make contact with one family to arrange for a time to meet and pray in their home.

It was Monday night and Dr. David knew he would have to lead the deacons' meeting on Tuesday evening. But Monday was his surgery day and he knew he would be tied up till late that night. Still, both he and Carol felt that in order to be good leaders, the remaining call should be made. Finally, on Monday afternoon, Carol reached the family by phone. They had been out of town but would look forward to a prayer visit from the Davids. The meeting finally took place—at 10:30 that night! Dr. David had been in surgery until 10:00, but he made it.

When he told me about his efforts just before the deacons' meeting, he was tired but smiling. He said, "You know, I just couldn't face those men and ask them to do what I had not yet done myself."

The question is, how do you find people who will lead like that? The answer is that God will put some people like that right in your path; do not overlook them. But for the most part you have to train them. The next obvious question is, how do you train them?

I learned that leaders lead, no matter what the cost, from the example of Captain Mack, that I related in Chapter 1. Without realizing it then, I had learned from him a biblical method. It was the way Paul taught Timothy: leading by example. The purpose in leading by example is not merely to set a standard by your conduct and performance for others to live up to and emulate. That itself is a noble cause.

Rather, the idea of leading by example has a progression factor in it—you get more done for the cause of Christ. It is a way of multiplying your efforts by getting more and more of God's people to learn how to do what the leader does by doing it! The apostle Paul put the principle in print: "And the things that you have heard from me among many witnesses, commit these to faithful men who will be able to teach others also" (2 Tim. 2:2).

The person who leads by example must be willing to put *time* into people. He must invest himself in whom he is training. Pastors and others who would train interns must not lose sight of the effort and priority of training someone else to do a job.

I have talked with many church leaders who have assumed mistakenly that getting seminary interns into the training program is a good way to get cheap labor. To approach the training of interns with that purpose in mind is to treat them unfairly. They will contribute mightily to the program, but the reason for having them is to train them for the future. The rule to follow here is this: if you do not have time to give them to train them, do not have them. It may seem expedient at the time to get people to do work that needs doing. But assigning tasks to untrained people brings frustration and anxiety to them—and to you.

A man once told about his first day on the police force in Minneapolis many years ago. With the notification that he was hired came the instruction to purchase his uniform and police revolver and report for duty on a certain day. He reported as ordered, expecting to begin a training course. Instead, the officer in charge gave him a badge, a whistle, and a night stick and said, "You take Hiawatha Avenue."

I am sure that does not happen on the police force in Minneapolis anymore, and it should not happen in the church. God's people can be trained to serve the Lord in His church in the same way that Paul trained Timothy. But it takes time, patience, loving concern, and an awareness of how the Paul-Timothy method works.

Four-part Formula

The Paul-Timothy method is more than teaching someone how the ministry works while in the classroom. It is based on a simple formula for training by example. It works if it is followed.

1. First you do the work and let him observe you.
2. Then he works with you.

3. You observe him as he works.
4. He works alone.

There is nothing of the aloof world of academia here. Paul put his life into Timothy and shared all that was dear to him of the ministry to which God had called him. A father-son relationship in the Lord developed and Paul called Timothy "my beloved son" (2 Tim. 1:2). Classroom studies are needed: but in order to do what Paul did for Timothy, there must be a warm, personal approach that urges, "Come with me, son, and I'll show you all I know."

First, Timothy observed Paul and Silas at Philippi. It was right after the young intern joined the ministry team. We pick up the story of Timothy in Acts 16:3, "Paul wanted to have him go on with him." Timothy readily accepted and began his lifelong journey in the ministry, following Paul that day. They went to Troas and then on to Philippi, where Timothy was to get his first big lessons in the ministry by way of observation. I will discuss that soon.

After a time, step two began. Timothy began to work with Paul as his helper and co-worker. We can see this in the way several of the epistles are addressed. Paul began his first letter to the Thessalonians, "Paul, Silvanus, and Timothy, to the church of the Thessalonians . . ." (1 Thess. 1:1). The letters to the Philippians and Colossians begin the same way, indicating that step two, "he works with you," was being followed. The latter two epistles were written when Paul was in prison the first time in Rome and Timothy was his right-hand man, probably in A.D. 61. Timothy worked alongside Paul, doing more and more. Soon he began to get assignments that gave him even more responsibilities.

124

As the ministry progressed, step three in the formula began, "you observe him as he works." Timothy began to do some of the work on his own as Paul observed him and encouraged him through letters. The first letter to Timothy was written when Timothy had taken up the assignment to oversee the church at Ephesus. We can see Timothy's assignments to Ephesus in Paul's instruction in 1 Timothy 1:3, "As I urged you when I went into Macedonia—remain in Ephesus that you may charge some that they teach no other doctrine." Paul's letter gave Timothy all of the basic information he would need to establish the churches. Timothy was doing the work and Paul was observing and instructing him.

This third phase is perhaps the most valuable time in a student's life. Once when I was working in this way with an intern, he chafed a bit under the instruction and discipline. He did not complain outwardly, but I could see that he was troubled and somewhat unhappy. With that, I took him aside and said, "Listen, son, this is a time to be thankful for. This will probably be the last time in your ministry when someone will sit down with you and tell you what you are doing wrong and how to correct it. There is an old saying, 'Only your friends will tell you.' This is it; I am telling you as a friend."

To learn by doing, and to have someone show you how to work and then coach you as you go along, is the best possible way to learn. That is why Paul could say, speaking of Timothy, "For I have no one like-minded, who will sincerely care for your state" (Phil. 2:20). Paul could be sure of Timothy's commitment and ability because he had poured his life into him. He had let Timothy observe him. He had involved the young man in the ministry with him. And then he observed Timothy while he did the work.

Finally, and sadly in this case, step four was reached, "he works alone." Paul was to be martyred and Timothy would carry on the work, bearing the responsibility for the apostolic ministry to the churches. Thus the four steps in the training formula—the Paul-Timothy method—were carried out.

What Did Timothy Observe?

We have already seen, in Paul's example, how important it is for leaders to give others examples of what they are expected to do. The idea that leaders lead, no matter what the cost, has to become part of our conscious efforts to lead God's people to do great things for Him. The old rule that says "Never ask anyone else to do what you won't do yourself" is as solid now as it ever was. I am convinced that ordinary people can do great things for God if they are led well and trained in the way Paul trained Timothy.

Admiral William Halsey said, "There are no great men, just ordinary men called upon to do impossible tasks." The admiral was not speaking of spiritual work necessarily, but what he said applies to it. The importance of leading by example, of having others observe the leader as Timothy observed Paul in step one, cannot be overstressed.

Let us go back now and look at exactly what Timothy observed at Philippi, when the young man got his first opportunity to see what the ministry really is and how God's men perform under fire.

1. He Saw Evangelists in Action.

The first thing the apostles did in Philippi was to win a woman named Lydia to Christ: "and when she and her household were baptized . . ." (Acts 16:15). Paul and Silas were evangelists, preaching Christ at every opportunity, planting churches as they went. The church at Philippi was begun that day.

Spiritual leaders should set the example in making Christ known. I have met far too many ministers who want to teach, counsel, or do administrative work and leave the evangelism to someone else. What is true for warfare is true for the spiritual war of the church: there are planners and there are fighters. In World War II, MacArthur was a planning general in the Pacific, while Wainwright and "Vinegar Joe" Stillwell were fighters. In Europe, Eisenhower was a planner, while Patton and Hodges were fighting generals.

It can also be argued that the church needs planners, but I can tell you that the men who do the actual fighting feel a lot closer to the fighters than they do to the planners. The trouble with God's army is that the Lord did not say anything about being a planning general or an armchair general. Instead we were told, "But you shall receive power when the Holy Spirit has come upon you; and you shall be witnesses to Me in Jerusalem, and in all Judea and Samaria, and to the end of the earth" (Acts 1:8).

A spiritual leader has to lead the way and do the very first thing every Christian is called upon to do. He must be a witness and be involved in the battle for the lives of men and women. No paper soldiers. No excuses!

2. He Saw Spiritual Answers Applied to Spiritual Problems.

When the demonic woman began to mock them, Paul used the spiritual power God made available to him. "But Paul, greatly annoyed, turned and said to the spirit, 'I command you in the name of Jesus Christ to come out of her.' And he came out that very hour" (Acts 16:18).

Too often we depend upon counselors, Christian or otherwise, to help people who really need spiritual deliverance. In seminaries, what is often taught for counseling is no more than what secular counselors learn in their schools. There is a need for biblical counseling and the church should provide it. At times pastors should refer counseling cases to professional help. But men and women of God should learn first to call upon God for spiritual help when help is needed; to apply spiritual answers to spiritual problems.

A pastor told of his experience in a case like that of Paul and Silas. A woman, with what looked to be a severe mental disorder, came in for pastoral counseling. It did not take the pastor long to know that he was over his head as far as normal counseling procedures go. But he went on to try to listen and discern her problem. As the woman talked, he became aware that a hateful attitude was beginning to show itself. Suddenly, it struck him! He was talking to an evil spirit. The pastor called in his associate, and the two of them prayed over the woman.

In relating the story to me, the pastor said, "I felt a little silly at first, but then I got my faith up and commanded the evil spirit to leave. To my amazement, the woman fell to the floor in a heap." Later, he said, the woman remembered nothing of the experience. But she was freed from her spiritual captor.

Other spiritual problems in the church should be dealt with in a spiritual way. Too often what seems political should be treated spiritually. In some churches democracy is so important that voting on an issue takes priority.

One church had a disturbance over how the Bible study groups should be managed. The practice had been to disband the groups after one year and reform them so cliques would not form and the people would get acquainted with more newcomers. One group leader strenuously resisted such regrouping and caused such dissension that the issue came to a vote at a church business meeting. The objector lost his case. It came out later that he was having a sexual affair with a woman in the group and wanted to keep her close to him. Hindsight is perfect here; in looking back the problem is easy to see.

In my own experience, such unreasonable demands usually have their roots in a moral problem or in bitterness. In this case, instead of letting the matter go to a congregational vote (of all things!), the pastor should have attempted to learn why the group leader felt so possessive about his group. Spiritual discernment was necessary, and that could only come through much prayer and soul-searching.

Personal confrontation is preferred to political upheaval, where innocent Christians can be unwittingly drawn into conflicts they do not understand. It has to be prayer and spiritual wisdom first, not politics. We can call upon the power of God to remedy any evil situation. Paul, when grieved by the mocking attack of the woman, brought God's power to bear on her by calling upon God to help. That was the example Timothy needed and remembered.

3. He Saw Good Soldiers.

Paul and Silas also showed Timothy their willingness to pay the price for the cause of Christ. There was no more important lesson to be learned.

The American attitude about suffering for Jesus is, "Let someone else do it, while I applaud." There is a kind of escape theology in the air that teaches us that if we hang on until the Rapture we can avoid trouble altogether. It is the idea that all we have to do is believe. Pain is to be avoided at all costs.

I do not know when the Lord is coming, but I do know that Christians need to be aware that they are in a fight! Spiritual warfare is real and everyone who serves Jesus Christ will share His sufferings. Our Lord told us this when He said, "Remember the word that I said to you, 'A servant is not greater than his master.' If they persecuted Me, they will also persecute you. If they kept My word, they will keep yours also" (John 15:20).

Timothy saw Paul and Silas face brutal punishment. When the men who made their livings by use of the demonic woman saw that she was healed, they were furious. The men of God were dragged into the marketplace where "the multitude rose up together against them; and the magistrates tore off their clothes and commanded them to be beaten with rods" (Acts 16:22). What must have impressed Timothy was how Paul and Silas continued to serve God even when a tremendous victory over their captors and their pain did not come. More than that, they worked on after the beating without considering the cost at all.

While visiting a church in San Diego, a young sailor demonstrated a willingness to face persecution and abuse for Jesus' sake, and he did it with a smile. He came in, flushed and excited, and told me of his experience on the bus en route to the church. Several other young men at first ridiculed him because he was carrying his Bible. Then they slapped him around and punched him. I could see where they had hit him. He did not complain. Instead he said with a big smile, "I have just been persecuted for Jesus. I feel great!" For the first time, he said, he felt like "a real servant of Christ."

The one who leads by example must be a good example; he must be willing to pay whatever price is required and pay it without whimpering.

4. He Saw Men of Genuine Faith.

"But at midnight Paul and Silas were praying and singing hymns to God, and the prisoners were listening to them" (Acts 16:25). Coach Vince Lombardi used to say, "When the going gets tough, the tough get going." Nowhere is that more true than in serving Christ.

The toughness of God's servants, however, lies in the rock-hard faith of the Christian who is absolutely certain God is with him. With this kind of spiritual leader, prayer is not a last resort. It is the starting point! Trusting in God is not what he does at the last minute, just as he bails out and pulls the rip cord. It is what he has going in! Timothy saw that Paul and Silas could pray and sing hymns, while their feet were in stocks and their backs were streaming blood from beatings. And when they prayed and sang hymns to God, He answered with an earthquake that set them free.

5. He Saw God's Men Keep Their Poise and Dignity.

What happened next must have surprised the magistrates. Paul and Silas would not leave like losers. When they were released and told to go in peace, Paul insisted on meeting with the authorities face to face. "But Paul said to them, 'They have beaten us openly, uncondemned Romans, and have thrown us into prison. And now do they put us out secretly? No indeed! Let them come themselves and get us out'" (Acts 16:37).

Like their Lord, these servants had not defended themselves when attacked. They could have claimed their rights as Roman citizens, but they did not. Then, after being freed from jail by God's hand, they had continued to evangelize, winning the jailor and his family. They claimed their rights as Roman citizens only to show God's power in them. What a lesson to learn! Do not panic when things go wrong. Do not rush to defend yourself. That will only get you in God's way. Keep your poise and dignity and let God work out the details.

It should be understood that when the trainee observes his teacher, he looks not only at the techniques and the task—he looks at his teacher as a person. He looks to see if his faith matches his profession. If the one being trained observes the qualities that Timothy found in Paul, both the student and his teacher will have passed the test.

These are some of the quiet qualities of leadership that should be observable in God's servants. If they are, then leading by example in the Paul-Timothy method makes them transferable as well.

Crucial Questions to be Answered

However, some leaders can set good examples, perhaps even matching that of Paul and Silas at Philippi, and still fail to lead by example in the fullest sense. Their failures come because they will not let those they train learn by actually working with them as in step two, "he works with you." And they fail again when they will not free their students to do the work themselves as in step three, "you observe as he works."

The first question that "Paul" in the Paul-Timothy learning situation must ask himself is, "Am I willing to let this Timothy fellow work alongside me?" Before this question is shrugged off, let us understand that not all will be willing to share what they do with others. Why? (1) For them it seems easier to do the work themselves than show others how to do it. (2) They might be insecure because they are not thoroughly trained in what they do and are embarrassed to let that be seen. (3) They might also be afraid to train others who might take their jobs. (4) Some enjoy working entirely alone. As loners, they are not accountable for their time to anyone. Having Timothys along would cramp their styles.

But the question here is, "Will the teacher let the student work alongside him?" To do that the teacher has to give himself to the student. And there is a cost to be borne by the teacher. He has to work patiently with a student who is going to make mistakes. Some are unwilling to endure the frustrations that can accompany such an undertaking. Others are simply unaware of the tremendous value at stake for the student.

That lack of patience and understanding sometimes can be seen when a father works on a project and his little son stands by, wanting more than anything to help his daddy do the work. A wise father will take the time to let his son learn to handle tools and even a paintbrush now and then. As the boy works alongside his father, he not only learns but feels a part of what his daddy is doing. As the son grows older, he learns more and more ways to maintain a home so that when he marries he will be equipped to care for himself and his family. The same is, of course, true for mothers and daughters.

However, there are men and women who will not let their children work with them. Children do not learn by merely observing; they must participate. So it is in the

Paul-Timothy method. The teacher must be willing to step aside and allow the student to do some of the work. He must carefully watch and evaluate what is being done and make corrections, remembering that mistakes are valuable. By making them, the student learns how not to make them again.

The real test comes when the student is ready to try his wings and do the work on his own, under observation, as in step three; you observe while they do the work. The teacher is still accountable for the outcome, but he takes his hands away and lets the student do the work.

That is akin to how a driving instructor feels when he has let the student driver observe him and then drive with dual controls, allowing the student to share in the process. When the instructor takes his hands off the wheel and lets the student go at it, he has both the joy of accomplishment and the anxiety that comes with observation. He can rejoice at his success in teaching the student how to drive. But he also feels distress watching for mistakes that can lead to trouble—accidents, I believe they are called!

There is risk in the Paul-Timothy method. The teacher has to believe that training another in the ministry of Christ is part of his calling and responsibility. And he has to have faith that the Lord Himself is also present in training sessions. Unless the teacher is willing to let the student work on his own, he is not being the Paul he ought to be.

Making It Practical

Here are some practical ways the Paul-Timothy method works in the church. (It is not a new idea, obviously, and many use it without giving it a name.)

In lay evangelism, the trainee will observe the trainer for a time. The evangelism team will make its calls with the teacher doing the talking and the student observing and praying. Then the teacher will ask the student to participate, perhaps talking to one person in a home while the teacher deals with another. The two may alternate calls and evaluate their work together after each one. Then the teacher will observe while the student carries the ball and completes the evangelism visit with no assistance except for prayer. Then he takes a student along and begins the same process. His work is thus transferable, and he can multiply himself and expand the ministry. He has a part in enlarging the kingdom of Christ.

As founding pastor of a church, I began with one man, making visits door to door in the area where the church was to be located. My partner, Jack Norman, was a new Christian then, but as he learned he was able to teach another new believer how to make evangelism calls. Soon, others were added as they became proficient enough to be leaders and teachers. The church was developed, and men and women were trained for ministering at the same time. This was the Paul-Timothy method.

In teacher training, the same method can be followed. The student observes, then participates in the work in the classroom, and then teaches under observation. Finally, when he is deemed capable, he is assigned to a class and begins to work on his own. He should be able to train another teacher as he was trained in the classroom.

We pastors must take seriously our responsibility of training and equipping others for the work of Christ. For too long the actual work of the pastor has been clouded by a variety of viewpoints and arguments over ministry styles. There is obviously a variety of ministries and different ministry styles. The Scriptures teach that. Whatever the style, we need to get on with expansion.

We especially need to multiply the workers in the fields, white unto harvest, in all of their varieties. It is God's will that we pray for workers to be sent into the harvest—surely He has heard all of our prayers. But we who are leaders in the church must be the instruments through which these prayers are answered. We need to train others who can work in the harvest field with us. God raises them up. God anoints them for the work. But someone with skin on his face has to lead by example and train others as Paul trained Timothy.

Sometimes pastors are deterred from training students for the ministry because of fear for their own jobs, induced by the silly remarks church members make. Often people will say to the pastor, "Oh, pastor, that young preacher is going to get your job. He is becoming so good at preaching." That is a foolish statement usually uttered in innocence by well-meaning Christians. Ignore such sayings. It does not pay to have rabbit ears and listen to every careless word uttered by people who do not know how they sound.

Once a parishioner told an intern who worked with me that he was doing so well he was sure to become an evangelist. Actually, the fellow could not preach his way out of an empty auditorium. But if an intern is doing well, and if the people love him and ask for him to preach, praise God! The Paul in the pulpit has done a good thing. He has produced a Timothy.

Let those who are disturbed by praise for their pupils know that if the ones they have trained succeed, they are a credit to their trainers. The congregation will know so, even if they do not say it. Pastors must not think of themselves as performers, but as workers and trainers. And the ones who are to be trained should be both lay leaders and people who will become pastors, teachers, and missionaries.

Often the only difference between lay leaders and professionals is that lay leaders have to support themselves with other jobs while professionals can give full time to the Lord's work. It is not enough occasionally to send a few men and women off to Bible schools and seminaries to be educated for the ministry. That is good, but the real training must be done in the local church.

The best way to train, and perhaps the only way, is to lead by example and be Paul to lots of Timothys.

Stand by Your Man

Few military leaders in the world's history have been as loved and venerated as was General Robert E. Lee. He was a brilliant leader and strategist who inspired the men who followed him as few others have. It was his care for those men that drew responses of love and loyalty. In times when they were outnumbered, outgunned, barefooted and hungry, the Army of Northern Virginia fought on valiantly. The American Civil War has long been history, but the memory of the Christian man who led the armies of the South is still with us.

Strangely, some of the very qualities that made him great have been looked upon as weaknesses. One critic said it kindly.

First, that he was too careful of the personal feelings of his subordinate commanders, too fearful of wounding their pride, and too solicitous for their reputation. Probably it was this that caused him sometimes to continue in command those of whose fitness for their position he was not convinced, and often led him, either avowedly or tacitly to assume responsibility for mishaps clearly attributable to the inefficiency, neglect, or carelessness of others. (from Walter

H. Taylor, *Four Years With General Lee* [New York: Bonanza Books, 1976], 146).

This is the beginning of a critique that in fact reveals some of Lee's strengths. Whereas it might be true that the beloved general overlooked the faults of some because of his concern for them, it is also true that it was a virtue not always seen in leaders. He stood by his men and was concerned for their welfare. As a result, they followed and fought superbly until Appomattox.

In fact, all true leaders seem to share Lee's qualities of leadership. They are able to surround themselves with other very capable people in order to accomplish important tasks. These leaders are like General Lee in that respect: they stand by their men. The umbrella man, the spiritual leader who is able to inspire others to follow him as he follows the Lord, will also have these qualities.

It should be seen clearly, however, that such qualities have their origins in Jesus Christ, who taught and practiced them. It is obvious that General Lee, who read his Bible and prayed daily, received these qualities or learned them from the Lord. It was his natural skill as a military commander—moderated and enriched by his spiritual heritage—that made him a great man.

When we look to Jesus, we see the source for all good leadership qualities. He taught us humility, the dignity of human life, what it means to be truly dedicated to a cause, and how to inspire others by example. By dying for us, He showed us how to be a friend. Jesus, our Lord, let us see that the battle to be fought here is worth the cost to us because of the hope victory promises.

In Chapter 4, I dealt with some qualities of spiritual leadership: accountability, responsibility, and humility.

Here, I want to set out principles of leadership that are rooted in these qualities.

1. Back up your man.
2. Always correct others in private.
3. Guard the dignity of those who follow you.
4. Follow the established plan.
5. Take the blame—share the glory.

These are basic leadership principles used in the military and in other secular organizations where they are understood. I have followed these principles for a long time because I know they work. Further, I have found them to be absolutely consistent with the teaching and example of Jesus. In fact, it is my opinion that they most likely have been taken from His methods of leadership. They are also what the church needs today! Every one of these principles benefits the follower and helps keep the church's mission on track.

Principle One: Back Up Your Man

"Back up your man" is a universal rule of leadership. There is nothing as motivating as knowing that whatever happens, your leader will stand by you and back you up when you need him. Likewise, there is nothing as demoralizing as getting into a tight situation, where you need support and backup, only to find your leader will vascillate and refuse to take responsibility for what he has assigned you.

The backup I speak of is exactly what the writer to the Hebrews meant when he said, "For He Himself has said, 'I will never leave you nor forsake you.' So we may boldly say: 'The LORD is my helper; I will not fear. What can man do to me?'" (Heb. 13:5–6). The assurance that Jesus gives us of His continuing presence and support is an article of faith for everyone who seeks to serve Him. That same kind of support and backup should be given to those who follow their leaders in the body of Christ. Jesus set the standard of leadership for us all.

Let us look at some situations where the one who is assigned a responsibility will need backup from his leader—when he has made a mistake, when others will not follow the plan as he directs, or when he is under attack and accused of wrongdoing.

I have found that it is good, as the leader, to establish the assurance of support and backup before any mistakes are made. In giving an assignment, I have found it helpful to say at the outset something like this: "Now that you understand the assignment, I want you to know that I expect you will make mistakes. Everybody does. Be careful to avoid mistakes, but don't be afraid if you make one. Let's learn by our mistakes on this project. Remember, I'll be here to help you through the thing, if a mistake occurs."

Actually, mistakes can be helpful if the leader can minimize the traumas and maximize the lessons learned from them. But anger at the cost of the mistake and the frustration of failure must be overcome.

One worker made a costly mistake that almost took his employer's life. Wisely, however, the employer turned the defeat around and made a victory out of it. He bore an initial loss, but the investment he made in his employee would pay off later. The employee was a young man who serviced two airplanes owned by his employer. One aircraft was a small executive jet, and the other was a conventional prop plane. While fueling the planes one day the young man was careless and reversed the fuel lines, putting kerosene into the prop plane which required gasoline, and pumping gasoline into the jet's tanks.

When the owner-pilot took off in the prop plane, he flew with no problem at all until he switched tanks and got kerosene fuel into his gasoline-powered engine. With that, the engine stopped. The pilot was able to make an emergency, wheels-up landing with significant damage to the airplane. The pilot was furious. He managed to have someone get him back to the airport and angrily looked for the young man who had almost killed him through negligence.

But when he saw his employee sobbing with grief at what he had done, the pilot relented. He put his arm around the young man's shoulder and said, "Son, from now on, no one but you is going to fuel my airplanes. I know that you will never make that mistake again." The young man was restored and became a better employee. Even costly mistakes can become beneficial if the leader can be supportive and if the hearts involved are soft.

Is that not how God leads us? Forgiveness and restoration are promised to the penitent. As 1 John 1:9 says, "If we confess our sins, He is faithful and just to forgive us our sins and to cleanse us from all unrighteousness." Most of us know that verse by heart. It is imperative that we leaders apply the same principle when dealing with others who have erred and are repentant. This kind of backup is essential to productivity and follows the example of Christ.

If a worker shows no concern about his mistakes, another course of action must be taken. He should be corrected or dismissed. If he is over his head in work and cannot do it all, he should be reassigned. The latter can be helpful to the worker if he feels supported in the transition.

Backup for a staff member who has to make a tough decision is also important. Tough decisions are frequent occurrences in the singles ministry, and the singles minister needs all the backup he can get. That is especially true when he has to deal with immorality in the group.

A member of the singles group came to me with a complaint about our singles minister. There was bitterness in his attitude as he told me how he had been banned from the group without cause. According to this gentleman, he had been misunderstood, falsely accused, and dealt with rudely.

After listening to his complaint, I asked the singles minister to come in and talk with us. As the three of us talked together, the real problem came to light. The man had been hounding some of the women in the group, even following them home from church to harass them and make lewd suggestions. Some of the women were frightened by him and had stopped coming to worship because of their fears. When I checked out the situation, I found it to be even worse than at first described.

The answer was obvious: I backed up the singles minister. The man was not allowed to attend the singles meetings, and the women were protected. But there will be other, more complicated problems that will require much prayer and wisdom in backing up your man.

If a staff member has acted unwisely and has made an error in handling a problem case, his error must be corrected. If the singles minister had been wrong in falsely accusing the man, another course of action would have been indicated. A pastor must act quickly to rectify a situation. He must care for the man who is wronged, but he must do so without making the staff member lose face or feel that others have gone over his head in going to the pastor.

If the singles minister in the case just described had unjustly accused the man in question, the minister would have had to correct his error. The mistaken staff member, in this case, would have gone to the man with an apology for his false accusation. The source of the bad information would then be dealt with and the man reinstated. Wisdom is called for in settling disputes, but the staff member who has to face these situations daily needs to feel that he is being supported, even when he has made an error. In fact, that is when he will appreciate it most.

However, backup most often fails when a staff member comes under attack and is falsely accused. The rule to follow here is clearly spelled out in 1 Timothy 5:19, "Do not receive an accusation against an elder except from two or three witnesses." That means do not even listen to the charge unless it is verifiable. Every man of God is susceptible to gossip and accusations. Facts must be presented and charges against the minister verified by witnesses if the charge is to be accepted.

I watched in horror from afar as a group of inexperienced deacons accepted such a charge against their pastor. The facts were that the pastor's wife was with him on a call in the very home of the woman who accused him of sexual advances. There were no witnesses to this accusation or to any other such sin in the man's life. However, instead of following Scripture and dismissing the charge as ridiculous, the board members followed an old proverb. They said, "Where there is smoke there is fire. The man must have done something wrong." With that the pastor was dismissed, his ministry ruined.

When a member of his staff is falsely accused, the umbrella man has to be willing to go to the wall with his man. He has to support him whatever the cost. If the staff man is not supported by his pastor, he has no support. His life and ministry are in jeopardy. If the pastor does not stand by his man, he can expect no support in return. But even worse than that, he will be contributing to the loss of one of God's servants.

A pastor once confessed to me how he failed to support his youth director when the young man was criticized for the way he dressed and for letting his hair grow a bit long in the manner of young people at the time. The pastor said, "I felt a little shaky in my own job at the time, so when the kid came under fire, I just threw him to the wolves. I let a committee handle it. The man is out of the ministry now, and I feel terrible about it."

What should the pastor have done to back up his man? First, he should have gotten the complainers and the youth minister together to discuss the problem. If it could not have been resolved, he should have supported the youth director, even to the point of suggesting that he liked the way he looked. There is always something wrong with that kind of complaint. People will pick on a man for the way he combs his hair when in reality they are unhappy about something else and cannot bring themselves to be honest.

I once sat with a pastor, at his request, in a congregational meeting at his church where his fitness for the pulpit was being judged. The most serious charge against him seemed to be that he sometimes wore a pink shirt, although it was obvious he was on trial for some other problem which the accusers never would mention. The pink shirt bothered them. "It didn't look ministerial," the complainers said. I wore a pink shirt to the meeting to support the man. It did no good.

The pastor who failed to back up his youth director was ashamed of himself for his lack of courage in failing to support his man when trouble came. I always think of Stephen at times like this and how comforted he was when he looked up and saw that his Lord was there to back him up in his moment of peril. "But he, being full of the Holy Spirit, gazed into heaven and saw the glory of God, and Jesus standing at the right hand of God" (Acts 7:55). No one who serves the Lord Jesus Christ will ever be forsaken by Him when in peril. Umbrella men, follow your Lord's example. Stand by your men.

Principle Two: Always Correct in Private

To correct a person's mistake in the presence of others is a grave injustice. First of all, the embarrassment of being publicly accused and corrected is a kind of punishment that has no place in Christian leadership. People who do correct publicly those who are responsible to them either do so out of anger or out of thoughtless neglect for the other person's well-being.

We have no record of Jesus' rebuking His disciples, except for the time when Peter resisted Jesus for speaking about His coming death. Even that was after Peter had taken Jesus aside, out of earshot of the others. It was then that our Lord said to him, "Get behind Me, Satan!" (Matt. 16:23).

The principle of correcting privately should apply in every leadership situation, whether it be in the home, in business, or in the work of the ministry. It is easy to become outraged at someone else's blunder, but to allow indignation to overcome one of the principles of spiritual leadership is sin. It is counterproductive. James, in speaking of this need, said, "Therefore, my beloved brethren, let every man be swift to hear, slow to speak, slow to wrath; for the wrath of man does not produce the righteousness of God" (James 1:19–20).

The problem of being judgmental in such cases is often caused by what I call the "ought to be's." People are forever saying, "They ought to be like this," or "They ought to be like that." My point is that people *be* like they are. We all have to accept this reality of life; people do not always behave well. It is no good being angry or judging others. We need instead to be helpful and understanding. Whatever goes wrong, the Christian leader should take the offender aside and correct him privately if correction is due.

What does a leader do when he knows to correct a brother privately but confronts him publicly in a moment of frustration? Most leaders have done that, including me. A student choir director was getting the sanctuary choir ready for the second morning service, just as I was winding down my sermon in the first service. But the director got the choir warming up early behind the platform and did it with three doors open. Just as the invitation was being given, the sound of ninety voices running up and down the scale came booming into the sanctuary. Somehow, I finished and closed the service. I went calmly, at first, up to the choir room. But when I got there, I confess I spoke more firmly than I had intended. After I left the choir room, the young director prayed with the choir and led them through the service without a hitch.

What did I do? First of all, I admired him greatly for

keeping his cool. But within minutes after the service closed, I put my arm around him and apologized for correcting him in front of his choir. Then on Wednesday evening as he rehearsed the group, I came in and apologized to them also and praised the director for his poise and commitment to his duty, which leads me to the next principle.

Principle Three: Always Guard a Person's Dignity

This principle is akin to private correction. The dignity God has given to every person should be revered and preserved. Ridicule is one of Satan's favorite weapons. It is almost foolproof, making even the bravest Christian lose his nerve.

Satan tried it on Paul and Silas at Philippi when the slave girl, possessed by a spirit of divination, mocked them. She followed them around, saying, "These men are the servants of the Most High God, who proclaim to us the way of salvation" (Acts 16:17). It did not work then, but it had a destructive force to it. Because ridicule is a weapon of Satan, it should never be used by God's people. The umbrella man must guard the dignity of everyone under the big umbrella in this regard, with equal consideration for everyone.

Jesus was careful to preserve even Judas Iscariot's dignity. His example shows us that we should always honor the dignity of another, even when he is in the wrong. That old saying, "Two wrongs don't make a right," is still true. In the upper room, on His last night on earth, Jesus washed all of the disciples' feet, including those of Judas. Then, when the time came, Jesus allowed Judas to leave the room and did not expose his betrayal to the disciples. Jesus simply told His betrayer, "What you do, do quickly" (John 13:27).

As with my mistake in correcting a young musician in public, if the leader makes a mistake, he must rectify it. He must guard the dignity of those who serve with him under his umbrella.

Principle Four: Follow the Plan

The commitment by everyone involved to follow the established plan is essential for success in every organization. In the military the rule is "Follow the last direct order." In battle, the requirement for adherence to this principle is absolute. Military history is filled with accounts of failures in battle because plans were not followed.

The second battle of Bull Run in the American Civil War is a classic case of such failure. General John Pope, commanding officer of the northern army, ordered a commander of twelve thousand veteran troops to move forward nine miles during the night to be in position for a morning attack. The commander, General Porter, ignored the command and allowed his troops to sleep through the night, effectively taking his force out of the important battle to be fought the next day. The northern army's loss at the second battle of Bull Run has been attributed in large part to this leader's failure.

Of that action, General Pope later wrote with some sarcasm, "What success might have been, if a corps of twelve thousand men, who had not been in battle that day, had been thrown against Longstreet's right while engaged in the severe fight that afternoon, I need not indicate" (*Battles and Leaders of the Civil War* [New York: Hawthorn Books, Inc., 1976], 226).

The umbrella man, engaged in spiritual warfare, must work to ensure that both leaders and followers are committed to the plan. Everyone must follow it.

We can see again the example of our Lord in establishing this principle for us. He stayed on schedule and never veered from his commitment or his timetable. Jesus carried out God's plan for our salvation. An example of His determination can be seen in Luke 9:51. "Now it came to pass, when the time had come for Him to be received up, that He steadfastly set His face to go to Jerusalem." Every leader must commit himself both to God's plan and the immediate plan of the local church where he serves. Spiritual leadership is a call to commitment. That example is established by our Lord Himself.

But the follower must be committed to his leader and beyond, to the Great Commander of us all. Once a plan has been worked out and assignments made, the follower must follow the last direct order. Over the years I have heard people who want to redefine the mission of the church. But good soldiers of Jesus Christ will follow the Commander's orders until we hear different from Him. That is what Paul meant when he said, "You therefore must endure hardship as a good soldier of Jesus Christ. No one engaged in warfare entangles himself with the affairs of this life, that he may please him who enlisted him as a soldier" (2 Tim. 2:3–4).

This, too, helps us to see how we should operate in the church. Whatever the plan may be, it should not be changed without informing all who are trying to carry it out. To ensure that the plan is realistic, these planners should not be advice-giving committees, but those who actually will do the work. Everybody has to follow the plan.

Principle Five: Take the Blame—Share the Glory

A leader often is blamed for the failure of the enterprise his group undertakes. This is so because he bears the ultimate responsibility for the work. To some, this taking of blame might seem cruel and unfair, and in some cases it might be so. A small company I know of went out of business because the market for its manufactured product failed, sending the company into bankruptcy. Some blamed the head of the company for failing to use good judgment. But there was no way for the man to anticipate the sudden downturn in orders for his product. He took the blame—and the loss.

However, when the leader understands that he will have to accept blame for the failure of his group, he will be much more interested in motivating people to become more efficient. Yes, the old "The buck stops here" idea has its benefits. When he understands it, the leader works harder.

A leader may be willing to take the blame, but is he willing to share the glory? Is he willing to share any praise? Often, leaders are praised while the people who do much of the work are ignored. A wise leader will see to it that those who work with him are amply rewarded with praise. I used to wonder why the enlisted men in my squadron always won all of the athletic events we played against our officers. The officers had some fine athletes among them, but they always lost. When a game was over, we enlisted men went away happy with our victory. Our leaders had helped us share a little glory, to enjoy a little praise.

Pastors and leaders must be careful to give praise to those who actually do the work. The umbrella man is worthy of praise for his work in equipping the saints and making opportunities for their service, but he must remember to encourage those under the umbrella and allow others to praise them.

Honoring the church, the body of God, honors and glorifies the head, our Lord Jesus Christ. There is an

The Umbrella Man as Decision Maker

There are several types of decisions the umbrella man has to make. The "go" decision is made in response to the known will of God. When the facts are clear and the will of God is known, no other decision is adequate. An affirmative response by those who would lead God's people is required in this case.

Then there is a "must know" decision, where the leader does not know the will of God. He must gather available information and find out what God wants done. When the time comes for the decision to be made, he must be decisive. He comes to a "go" or "no go" point and must decide.

Finally, there is the work of the decision-making group, where we see the "process of decision making." However, in all of these, prayerfulness, decisiveness, and faithful obedience to the Lord are required. Let us look first at what I call the go decision.

The Go Decision

There was a big difference in the ways Moses and Joshua led the people of God. The most obvious difference was the way they made their decisions about entering the promised land. Moses, great leader that he ultimately was, listened to what the people said. Joshua, on the other hand, knew what God wanted done and was bound to do it. Moses sent an unorganized committee of twelve to spy out the land; Joshua sent in two hand-picked men. Moses sent the spies out to see if the invasion would work; Joshua was not concerned with if it could be done, but how God wanted it done. Both men needed to make go decisions, but only Joshua came through. Let us look more closely at what happened.

General Moses

The story of Moses, leading the new nation, Israel, out of Egypt in the Exodus is well-known. His celebration with the people on the far shore of the Dead Sea was short-lived, however. At Kadesh-Barnea, Moses chose twelve men to spy out the land. But the report of what they saw spelled defeat for the venture even before it could be launched. The spies made the common mistake of maximizing the strength of the enemy and minimizing their own God-given strength and power. As it worked out, Joshua and Caleb were the only spies who believed that God would give them victory. They pleaded for the invasion to begin. They believed that God would go before them.

When I said Moses sent out an unorganized committee, I meant that he apparently did not give them proper instructions. And it is obvious that they were not well-motivated. I do not like to fault Moses, and hindsight is perfect (these accounts were written for our instruction), but either his choice of leaders was poor or Moses did not tell the spies of the Lord's intentions. In Numbers 13:2, the Lord spoke to Moses with these instructions: "Send men to spy out the land of Canaan, which I am giving to the children of Israel; from each tribe of their fathers you shall send a man, every one a leader among them."

There was no question about God's plan; He was going to give Israel the land before them. However, some Christian leaders today would argue that Moses did right in letting the committee go in without clear direction regarding God's instructions. Certainly, such a committee must be affirmed in its choices. A leader would want to give the committee members freedom after all, to make their own decisions without the leader's sharing his information or exercising his authority.

When the one God has put in leadership knows the will of God without question, he is obligated to make that will known. This is not merely a question of the leader's authority. What is in question here is obedience to the will of God when the will of God is clearly known.

I think part of Moses' problem was the effect of his unrelenting problems with the people. God had given him seventy elders to help him, but then the people complained about the food and God gave them quail to eat. *Lots* of quail! Then with the quail came a plague. It was a disaster. After that Aaron and Miriam rebelled against their brother. Finally, God intervened to affirm Moses and punished Miriam with leprosy, but all of this must have taken its toll. (See Num. 11–12.)

My point here is this: a tired, beleaguered, and frustrated leader has trouble making a go decision. In light

155

of this we should take seriously the words of the late Vince Lombardi, the great football coach, who said, "Fatigue makes cowards of us all."

Perhaps Moses should have been alone with God for a few days before sending the spies into Canaan. I used to know a pastor who would spend one night a month out on the Southern California desert. If the weather was good, he would sleep outdoors under the stars, resting and communing with God.

Knowing the Lord's purpose and will as he did, Moses should have told the spies to go in and find ways and means to approach and defeat the enemy. But the question of whether or not there should be an invasion should not even have been on the agenda. A go decision already should have been made by faith. But instead of listening to God and giving firm direction, Moses allowed a committee report to change God's plans for Israel.

In fairness to Moses, another explanation might be that Moses did give the spies instructions and they simply refused to obey. Perhaps because they lacked faith and hearts for God, the ten spies just caved in and quit when they saw the enemy. Still, I think Moses' utter frustration and fatigue showed through. No one can blame him. Even God finally gave up on the faithless people and let their carcasses fall in the desert.

General Joshua

With Joshua everything was different. Forty years later the invasion was up to him. The man who pleaded with Moses for a go decision must have been frustrated for all the forty years of wilderness wandering. Finally, though, when the time came, he was ready. This time, he had motivated people who had suffered from their fathers' failure of faith. They had grown up wandering in the desert. At last Joshua received the word: it was "go."

Notice he did not send out twelve spies. He sent only two! And he sent them out without fanfare. They went secretly as we are told in Joshua 2:1, "Now Joshua the son of Nun sent out two men from Acacia Grove to spy secretly, saying, 'Go, view the land, especially Jericho.'"

We are not told much about them, but they were men of faith and God was with them. It is noteworthy that they reported directly to Joshua, not to the congregation of Israel. And they brought a good report. For them, the question of go or no go was never an issue. They knew they were going to take Jericho. The only question was how.

Those who lead the flocks of God today are sometimes more like Moses than Joshua; they often have to lead people who do not want to be led. When Christians get into the habit of sitting and listening instead of actively serving, they do not want to move ahead. The church becomes like a train with flat wheels. It takes a big shove to get it going.

A pastor who leads a growing and exciting church told me, "When I started with the church, the people had no vision and no heart to work. Things are great now, but I had to drag the church, kicking and screaming to victory. Only God and I know how hard I had to preach and prod to get things going."

He had made a go decision. For that pastor there was no other direction, no other decision that could have been made. He knew that he had to get the church going. Even though he was the only one who knew what God wanted, he had to act decisively. Getting people to do what God has decided for them is part of the leader's job in the decision-making process. It has never been easy nor has God told us it ever will be.

That is why the voice of the prophet must be heard again in the church. The one who expounds the Word of God to the church must be able and willing to say, "Thus saith the Lord," and then explain what must be done to accomplish the Lord's will. But he had better be sure the will of God has been made clear to him.

It is easy to say, "The Lord spoke to me and told me this," or, "I saw a vision." Let those beware who make such claims. God's warning in Deuteronomy 18:20 is still in force, "But the prophet who presumes to speak a word in My name, which I have not commanded him to speak, or who speaks in the name of other gods, that prophet shall die."

Every word the preacher speaks in these matters should be the proclamation of the Word of God. His "Thus saith the Lord" must be the exposition of the Bible. He must not apply Scripture to his experience but must experience the Scripture. This is because experience can be counterfeited. The Word of God does not exist because we have experiences. It is the Word of God because He said it.

Today's Generals

What, then, is a typical go decision for a pastor today? It is one made when he is certain without a doubt that he knows God's will. For instance, if he finds in Scripture that he is to equip the believers for service, he must move to do that. How it is all worked out may be decided in part by those who work with him. But the pastor who sees it as a go decision will begin to disciple the believers, both to equip them and give them opportunities for service.

When he sees in Scripture that every Christian is to be a witness, he must lead the church in that direction. He will meet opposition; but if he knows he is in the will of God, he will train those who are willing. Others can follow later. When the pastor finds that stewardship is a great part of the life of the church and must be taught, he must make the decision to teach stewardship throughout the church.

The umbrella man must not be discouraged if many of God's people are willing to sit back and watch him work. Instead, he must help them see that they should be doing the work of the Lord. I mentioned earlier that the pastor is not the hired gun. This is a figure of speech we in the West have used to depict the fellow who was hired to deal with anyone who needed shooting. Here, the hired gun is the paid agent who does all the shooting for Jesus.

Many people in the church have the idea that when it is time to witness to a neighbor, or when someone is sick and needs assistance, it is time to call the pastor. After all, that is what he gets paid for. Without knowing it, they have subscribed to the hired gun idea. It takes considerable teaching to help God's people see that they can be equipped to minister as well. The pastor will be ready to help and to serve. In many cases, church members can have the joy of actually being shepherds to others themselves. In this way, the body of Christ is better cared for and the church is built up.

Instead of leaving the church in the hands of an unorganized committee, the umbrella man must act on his go decisions when he knows God's will and must take as many along with him as possible, praying that others will follow. It takes time and perseverance to accomplish all that God wants done, but nothing can happen until a beginning is made. That is what umbrella men do: they make beginnings and then expand what is begun.

The Must-know Decision

The "must-know" decision is one that requires the leader to seek the will of God for a specific question. The group process comes later. This is a situation where the umbrella man must find out for himself what the will of God is. In some cases, he can find out what he needs to know by making inquiries. For example, when there is trouble, the leader must know the nature and the extent of the problem. To act impulsively at such times can bring on even more trouble.

Every spiritual leader will have complaints and problems to solve, just as Moses did. But before he decides on a course of action, he must define the problem. What is the complaint? How many are involved? Who are the leaders? If the complaint is legitimate, what can be done to rectify the situation? If there has been a misunderstanding, how can it be clarified? If he is facing a rebellion, the leader will have to decide how to confront the problem. A wise decision maker will find out what he must know and then, after much prayer, do whatever must be done.

The apostle Paul had a must-know situation regarding the status of the church at Corinth. He needed to know how the church had received his instructions about dealing with immorality in the church. But he seems to have been concerned about his previous letter. Was he too heavy-handed? Would the church continue to accept his authority as an apostle?

Paul waited in Macedonia while Titus went to Corinth to see how things were there. When Titus returned,

Paul was pleased. In 2 Corinthians 7:6–7, he wrote, "Nevertheless, God, who comforts the downcast, comforted us by the coming of Titus, and not only by his coming, but also by the consolation with which he was comforted in you, when he told us of your earnest desire, your mourning, your zeal for me, so that I rejoiced even more."

The apostle had delayed any plans for visiting Corinth again until he could know the situation there. He was free to communicate again by letter and plan for a third visit. His decision had to wait until the must-know part of it had been supplied with adequate information.

The most important part of the must-know decision comes through prayer. Prayer enables the spiritual leader to seek God's will in quiet solitude with Him. It is important to make inquiries and gather information, but the one who seeks to know the will of God must pray. I have found that the answers to my questions in prayer do not always come immediately. I try to pray over a period of days, or even weeks if it is possible. Then as the puzzle begins to unravel, as God leads, I seem to know the way to go. It seems to be an intuitive kind of knowledge but one I do not have before I pray.

Prayer can bring two believers together on a question so that they know God's will. When Derk Van Konynenburg was wrestling with a must-know decision, seeking to know what his part should be in the church's mission program, his question to God was whether or not he should be used in his local church as a half-time volunteer. Derk was willing; but before he volunteered, he wanted to be sure his decision was God's will.

Part of his prayer was for the pastor to be willing to launch the church on a more expansive world outreach. He and I had not yet talked together about missions, but

I had begun to feel the Lord's leading me to do more in world missions. A few weeks after Derk began praying, I announced my conviction from the pulpit.

After the service Derk was smiling. He said, "Pastor, God has just answered my prayer." With that, he began to explain about his need to know the will of God for his life and how God had apparently worked in both of us to make His will known. Derk has been leading our world outreach ministry ever since with great effectiveness.

Prayer in decision making has to be learned and experienced. It requires the experience of seeking God and finding Him willing to reveal His will and give His wise counsel about how to accomplish it. But learning happens through doing.

When I was a new pastor and still going to seminary, I knew an older, retired minister who was very poor in worldly goods. But he was a very prayerful man. One time he told me about his prayer life. He said, "We must seek God's will, so I pray about every decision I make." To make his point clear, he added, "I even pray in the morning about which necktie I should wear. I ask God for a decision about even a small thing like a tie."

Being rather foolish, I thought to myself, "I can't believe that the God who made the rainbow would choose neckties like this man's!" But then I realized that he was sharing a great truth with me, learned over years of service for the Lord. I understood that what the old pastor really was trying to say was not about neckties. He was really telling me to learn to pray and find the answers from God's throne, for my must-know decisions. The old pastor was a man of prayer who was not as poor as he looked. He was right about seeking God's guidance in decision making.

Too many of us rush through life, making decisions on the spur of the moment. In fact, some of the most important decisions in our lives are made that way. Human nature is impulsive, and because of that we need to seek God's wisdom in decision making. Umbrella men must take great care to make every decision a spiritual decision, because decision making is a spiritual process. Impulsive decisions, based on human intuition alone, can spell disaster for the pastor and the church he leads.

A pastor was fired by his congregation for poor leadership. He was a good preacher. His personal life was an example of godliness and servanthood. Furthermore, he had been pastor of the church for many years. What, then, brought about his downfall? He was impulsive when it came to hiring staff. Without adequate prayer and without careful examination and consultation with others, he would recruit and hire staff members who invariably failed—several because of moral problems.

His impulsiveness did him in. He mistook his human impulses for God's approval. This pastor failed to see that the decisions he was making were really must-know decisions. Unfortunately, he acted in haste, not gathering adequate information and failing to pray and give prayer time to work in his life.

Often Christian leaders fail to differentiate between how they feel and what God has caused them to know. This is when they become impulsive. Prayer is the best way to avoid human impulsiveness. Prayer is powerful. It brings the Lord of the church into the decision-making process. Prayer helps us to understand better our real problems as we lay out the details before the Lord. Then, with patience, we wait upon Him to help us digest the facts before us. In time He gives us His answers. Prayer is a process by which God communicates with us individually and with others in the decision-making process.

The Group Decision

Some of the most important decisions made in the church are rendered by decision-making groups. The work of these groups in making policy decisions and action decisions will spell success or failure for the ministry. Therefore, the attention we give their work here is very important.

First of all, the selection of decision makers should be carefully undertaken. Unhappily, in many churches the nomination of those who will make decisions for the church is done almost at random. Church members often choose uncommitted and unqualified people to make extremely important decisions for them, without considering what the Bible says about the selection of leaders. In Chapter 5, I discussed the qualifications listed for bishops and deacons. I believe that all who make major decisions for the church should meet the same qualifications. If they do not, the failure of the group is assured.

I was once asked to sit in on a deacons' meeting in a church where I was a guest preacher. As the meeting convened, there was obvious tension in the air. Before long, one man, the senior member of the board, began to object to what was being said by others. Soon he was in a rage! He quickly destroyed all hope of accomplishing anything in the meeting by his outbursts. Embarrassed, I quickly excused myself from the meeting, but later I found that it was quite a normal evening for the group.

The oldest member of the board had acted in a group-destroying role. He seemed to be unable to consider the opinions of others, but he was highly regarded because he was a professional man in the community. We have to learn that a person's professional skills in one area of life do not qualify him for the spiritual arena. No one is qualified to serve as a decision maker for the Church of Jesus Christ, unless he meets the spiritual qualifications in the Word of God. Great care must be taken in selecting decision makers.

I have found a solution to the problem that has worked extremely well. First, requirements for decision makers should be established. Then, instead of having nominations open on the day of the election of officers, people can be given as much as two weeks to submit nominations in writing to the nominating committee. The committee then will have the opportunity to qualify each candidate or disqualify those who do not meet the requirements established. It can all be handled confidentially so that no one will be embarrassed. While not foolproof, this method works well. I have used it for twenty-seven years with great results.

When the apostles and the elders met in the council at Jerusalem (probably in A.D. 50), they introduced a new method of decision making for the church. Their way of prayerful group decision became the model for later councils of the church, and certainly a model for us. No longer did the disciples cast lots to know the will of God as they did to find the replacement for the fallen Judas Iscariot.

Filled with the Holy Spirit, they gathered to discuss the issue before them and resolve it. Their aim was to find the will of God by hearing what He was saying to each member of the group. The process required everyone to be heard. And in the process of prayerful discussion, those men, all of them with strong views, came to know and follow God's will regarding the Gentile converts. In Acts 15:28, James, the overseer of the Jerusalem church, summarized the decision of the group: "For it seemed good to the Holy Spirit, and to us, to lay upon you no greater burden than these necessary things." Today, the decision-making group should follow the same process. Informed and prayerful, each member will be involved in thoughtful discussion, with the judgment rendered by the leader.

However, in order to be free to speak what he actually is thinking, it will be necessary for each participant to be able to separate the subject he is debating from any personalities. I call this separating the method from the motive. That means focusing on the issue and *objectively* discussing it. If we understand that the motives of the group members are not in question and that merely the issue is being discussed, then all can speak freely. This seems all too clear, but the question of people's motives often is misunderstood.

In talking to members of our official board at the orientation we hold each January, we always discuss the group process and how we must separate our motives from the methods under discussion. I have been amazed to see how businessmen latch on to this idea. We hold up one hand like a catcher's mitt and slap the imagined pocket to illustrate to one another that we are speaking about the issue and not the motive of the speaker. It is as if to say, "Go ahead and shoot. I can be objective because I know you are talking about my argument and not about me."

An aeronautical engineer, after we had practiced this

in the board meetings, told me that he had received two promotions because of it. He said, "After I learned that when I heard criticism on the job, I knew they were talking about airplanes and not about me, I could listen."

In order to know God's will, those who serve in a decision-making group must be careful not to dominate, but to contribute to the whole. Everyone must share in the process. As issues are discussed and proposals are made, the idea is for everyone in the group to participate. Each member must be adequately informed about the matter to be decided. And everyone must pray and come prepared to seek God's will through discussion with others.

It must be a process, not a personality. Prayer, contemplation, and thoughtful conversation must be the way of the group, not the domination of one over others. Most of us do not need an example, but here is one that helps to illustrate what I mean by the need for a process and not a personality.

In one church a very domineering woman ruled the women's work. She was powerful in personality and ruthless with criticism and rebuke. When church business meetings were held, she would intimidate the women in the church into voting with her, usually against progress. Because the church voted with a show of hands, she could see who opposed her and go after them with verbal abuse if they got out of line. These were genuine terror tactics. Finally, the church leaders changed the voting from a show of hands to a secret ballot. The process of decision making thereby continued.

A second example is more common. Three good men prayed, worked, and gave to found a new church in an

167

expanding neighborhood. In order to ensure orthodoxy, they established themselves as permanent elders and decision makers. Soon a pastor was called and the church began to grow. Progress went well for several years until the permanent elders began to protect what they had developed instead of thinking creatively and bringing changes to meet changing needs. One elder died and another became disabled as the years went by.

The remaining elder saw himself as protector. New elders were added, but he dominated them—and the pastor. It seemed to be *his* church. There was no decision-making process, just his personality. This situation was not happily resolved. The pastors came and went. The elders served in name only. The church died!

During a discussion, all kinds of objections can be raised. But after the decision is made, all should support it in unity. They should be in complete agreement that they have found the will of God. Hopefully, all will see what God is saying and agree. While unanimity is ideal, sometimes all will not agree. So then, if there cannot be unanimity, there must be unity. As in the council at Jerusalem, once the discussion is over and a decision is made, each one in the group should be willing to yield to the consensus. Each member must be accountable to the group, willing to comply with its decision.

The discussion should end with everyone committed to support the decision so prayerfully and thoughtfully made with the help of the Holy Spirit. Those disagreeing should say, "I will go with the group and we will have unity on the decision." No one should say, "I didn't vote for that, so I'm not going to do it!" Just as judges and lawyers view the legal process to be binding, so should staff, board, and other decision-making groups in the church regard this decision-making process as sacred. It seeks to know what God is thinking by finding out what God is saying to each one in the group.

CHAPTER • ELEVEN

The Accountability Group

While he was mayor of Modesto, Peter Johanson spent virtually every weekday morning meeting with other businessmen in discipleship groups. In our city the mayor serves without pay, so Peter had to operate his floor-covering business while serving as mayor and leading the early morning discipling ministry in restaurants around the city.

Then he would arrange a luncheon appointment with a nonbelieving businessman and a man from one of the groups. The luncheon met two needs. First, the gospel was given to the unbeliever as one man talked and the other man prayed. Second, it gave the man from Peter's discipling group the new experience of sharing his faith to one of his peers. It was quiet work for the Lord that produced many Christian leaders for the churches of the town and many new Christians for the kingdom.

I met Peter Johanson when I arrived in Modesto. He was a member of the church but was unable to use his discipling skills there. The church leaders looked upon Sunday school as the only place for discipleship. The real problem was that the spiritual climate in the church would not permit such changes.

I have already described my struggles to raise the spiritual umbrella and see a spiritual breakthrough. What I did not know was how beautifully Peter's discipling ministry was going to fit under that umbrella. However, when the time came to add a minister of evangelism and discipleship to the staff, I realized that we had almost let Peter get away from us.

Our small staff agreed that we should ask Peter Johansen to join us in that position. We felt that God was calling him to full-time service. As we prayed and talked about it, I felt a sense of urgency. I knew I needed to see Peter right away. That very moment I telephoned Peter and asked to see him at his store. He was no longer mayor but was still an extremely busy man.

In the brief time we had together, I asked him if he had ever considered a call to the ministry. To my amazement, he answered, "Yes, I have. In fact, I have arranged to sell my part of the business and follow the Lord's call." He explained that he had planned to serve with one of the large parachurch ministries.

Then it was Peter's turn to be amazed, when I told him why I was there. Later, he accepted the call to serve on the pastoral staff, giving full time to his work of evangelism and discipleship in the church. The breakfast meetings and noontime lunches in restaurants around town would continue and be expanded. We wanted to make Peter's outreach the church's ministry. It would be the beginning of the kind of discipleship that would help us to establish and expand the Lord's work. From these ideas, our accountability groups in the church were born. The big umbrella was up at last, and an important under umbrella, which has changed many lives, was established under it.

Peter's story shows the importance and necessity of

the umbrella man's work. The church often is not able to accept what God wants to do for and through His people because the spiritual climate will not permit it. It is up to the pastor to make the spiritual breakthrough and establish a healthy environment under the umbrella he erects.

The church needs to expand its vision and extend its outreach through all kinds of ministries waiting to be developed. The accountability group is just one of these, but it is a ministry that can develop mature Christians. There are three basic kinds of groups which can be developed, with variations according to the need.

The Home Bible Study Group

The accountability group that is best known in our church is the home Bible study group. Each is made up of twelve to fourteen people who commit themselves for a period of time, usually one year or more, to the discipline of the group. They agree to attend faithfully and participate each week, meeting in various homes as they rotate the location.

Five areas of endeavor are involved. First is the commitment to Bible study, using a study book as a guide. Prayer, memorization of Scripture, fellowship, and outreach fill out the requirements. The leader is not a teacher but a guide, who holds everyone accountable and seeks to keep everyone involved. The accountability is accepted readily and is really no more than saying, "I will be a good member of the group. I will participate faithfully."

Church leaders who are afraid to ask their fellow Christians to join them in being accountable should look at what the civic clubs and lodges demand of their members. Even the local bowling league makes the church look weak by comparison. Ask a bowler to come to a meeting on his bowling night and he will say, "I am sorry. That's my bowling night and we are in the league. The team needs me."

I do not fault that one bit. The team does need him and he ought to be there. The church's problem, though, is that God's people have not been made to feel that what they do for Jesus Christ in His church is important. Leaders have been afraid to ask for commitment. One church member told me, "I am glad to know that I am needed. You know, pastor, for so long around here, it didn't seem like anything important was going on. No one required me to do anything. This group is the best thing that has happened to me in years."

Others in the groups are thankful for their faithful Bible study because they are accountable to the group for their lessons each week. The same is true of Scripture memorization, prayer, and the other requirements. If the idea of being accountable stretches you, think of the weight-watching or exercise groups that make members account to one another. Accountability is a healthy, motivating force in our lives if we are accountable to the right people and involved in the right disciplines.

In these groups, the accountability becomes more enjoyable and less formal as the group progresses. Members pray for one another and actually begin to feel responsible for their brothers and sisters in the group as they never have before. An older church member, who enjoyed his faith more than ever because of his involvement in a group, said, "There is so much love in this group. We really do care about each other and we help

173

one another in so many ways. Thanks for coming up with this program."

Out of these home Bible study groups, our basic accountability groups, come the leaders of the church. In the process of guiding the group, the conducter looks for people who show promise as future leaders. We started with one group and happily saw two leaders emerge. After some training, they went on to be group leaders themselves. It should be remembered that leadership in the groups is all-important. Those who remember the old cottage prayer meeting idea will remember that many times those groups deteriorated into gossip sessions or worse.

Leaders for the accountability groups must be well-chosen. Actually, those who lead such groups become undershepherds, helping the pastors to care for the flock; so, their selection and training is vital.

A pastor I know decided to start twenty such groups at once. He had no trained leaders and lacked the skills to lead such a group himself. The obvious happened. All twenty groups failed and the program died. The old "We tried it once and it didn't work" cry was loud and clear from then on. The first group *has* to fly. That is why I recommend starting small and then expanding as good leaders become available. We usually have a waiting list of people who want to get into groups, but I would rather wait for leaders than see the groups fail.

There seems to be a moving of God's Spirit across the church that is leading God's people to want to be more accountable. That is why I stress the need for leaders to be willing to ask for that accountability. But the leader must be the first one out of the chute. He must be willing to be accountable, too.

The Discipling Group

The discipling group is a more intensive accountability group. Here is the story of one such group and what resulted. A medical doctor and a businessman began to meet for prayer and Bible study. Soon the group began to grow and the men became accountable to one another in an openness and kind of transparency that was new to all of them.

In preparing to write this chapter, I interviewed four of the twelve men who were in that early group in 1968. They were easy to reach because, like Peter Johansen, all four of them are now serving with me on our pastoral staff. Walter C. "Bud" LaCore was in the tire business and is now our business administrator. Jerry Collins is the head of adult ministries, which includes evangelism and discipleship. He was formerly a jet fighter pilot and then a salesman. The case of Derk Van Konynenburg was a bit different. Derk is a farmer who gives his time to serve on staff as the director of the world outreach ministry. Jim Talley, who first came to Modesto as a civil engineer on a dam building project and then went on to complete his theological education, is our minister to singles.

All four men look back to that early group as the place where they began to become accountable to the Lord. The next step, to give their lives for service, was not difficult after that. For these men, the discipling group was a place to share their lives openly in a bond of confidence that drew them together. At each meeting they maintained the discipline. The first one to arrive at the restaurant would begin to read his Bible and then share what he was reading with the next man who came in. This eliminated small talk and started them immediately in their sharing together.

Before prayer, they talked about their own needs. They began to answer to one another for their behavior. At one meeting, for example, they determined together to obey the civil law. That sounds strange coming from a group of upright citizens, but they were serious about it. Their discussions included questions about income taxes, hiring illegal aliens, using pesticides that were banned, obeying speed limits, and the need to tell the truth. In all of these matters and more, they committed themselves to complete honesty. It was life-changing.

Their discussions moved on to include the care of the family, husband and wife relationships, performance on the job, stewardship of all that belongs to God, and their own ministries in their local church. In all of this, their Bible studies and discussions turned to holiness and commitment to the Lord for service. Most of all, they committed themselves to the Lord and His Word.

Other men, some of them not yet Christians, were invited to the group and a number of them became believers. Lee Roddy, who has been such a help to me in writing this book, became a Christian in the group at that time. Now, virtually everyone who participated in that first discipleship group is serving the Lord. Some are now ministers, and others are very responsible lay leaders. The discipleship groups we operate in our church were patterned after this model.

The Advanced Discipling Group

The advanced discipling group is a select group of people who are chosen by the leader and invited to participate. They are people with high leadership potential who have already been involved in home Bible study groups and discipleship groups. This group, like the others, can be designed for men, women, or couples. In the group I will describe, we begin with the men and then ask their wives to participate with them.

When a potential leader is asked to participate, his willingness to come faithfully to an early morning meeting will be the first test of his commitment. For the benefit of those who find presunrise meetings a bit difficult, let me say that I am not a morning person either. For those like me, early rising, often after a busy night, is a test of our willingness to become truly accountable to a group. I do not think there is anything spiritual per se about getting out early in the morning. It is the discipline that counts.

There are no ABC's to the working of this kind of group, no established formula. The program has to be tailor-made to fit the needs of the people in the group. However, basic areas are covered in one way or another in each of these groups. They include being answerable to God's will in one's (1) marriage, (2) job, (3) church, and (4) personal life.

Selecting Group Leaders

What should you look for in selecting members for this group? We often make the mistake of thinking the bright person can lead without further qualifications. Do not look first for a high IQ. It is nice to have one but you do not have to be really brilliant to do what the Lord wants done.

The emphasis has to be on willingness to serve. The key to effectiveness is servanthood and Spirit power. Remember what Paul said to the Corinthians about their qualifications, "For you see your calling, brethren, that not many wise according to the flesh, not many mighty, not many noble, are called. But God has chosen the foolish things of the world to put to shame the wise, and God has chosen the weak things of the world to put to shame the things which are mighty" (1 Cor. 1:26–27).

The Servant Quotient

What is wanted is not so much an "A" student but a man or woman of faith with a servant's heart. We call that the "SQ" or "Servant Quotient." How much is the person willing to serve Christ and the church rather than himself? Will he lead as a servant, or will he become a tyrant? A servant will see himself as part of a larger group, contributing to the good of the whole. A tyrant will see himself as outside the group but in command, with his own best interest at heart.

Every one of us has a motor driving him from within—call it motivation. If the SQ is missing, all of the skills in the world will not make a leader. Hopefully, if a person with a servant's heart makes himself accountable on this level, he can become an effective and productive leader in the Church of Jesus Christ.

Time Management Survey

The groups begin with a time management survey. We have used it in every accountability group. How a person uses his time will indicate his values and interests. The survey provides a window that indicates what has to be changed to make his spiritual life more effective.

A woman came for counseling about family problems. Her marriage was about to break up and she was distraught. An attempt was made to get her and her husband to become more active in the church, but she said, "I'm too busy for that!" Finally, her marriage did fail. Her home was broken. Then she came back for counseling and was willing to work at some solutions.

Her assignment was to fill out a time management survey, included in this chapter. After one week, she came back and announced, "I've found my own problem." She was amazed to discover she was spending almost two hours on the phone every day and over four hours watching television. The most creative hours of her day were spent in idleness. But she did not realize how her time was being spent until she did the survey!

People who want to learn to be leaders need to manage their time well. But unless they make themselves accountable for their time, they may honestly not know how they are spending it. "Spending time" is a common term, but it is accurate. Time is valuable. Responsible leaders will learn to spend it well—or better still, redeem it.

The Relationship of Husband and Wife

How a man treats his wife is of first importance, and he can get a lot of help when he is willing to make this an area of accountability. In the advanced group, the husband should be discipling his wife. But let us include here the question that should be asked earlier. Do the husband and wife pray and read and discuss the Bible together?

A. W. Tozier's book, *The Pursuit of God,* can be recommended as a way to begin worship and Bible reading together in the home. Most people who are not used to reading the Bible and commenting together on it will bog down. This book will help to make discussion and prayer easy and more natural. If the husband is to become a leader, however, he must lead in his own home.

Couples should develop a life goal. This is a key to spiritual development in a marriage. One couple asked, "How can we serve the Lord better? We're going to church, involved in ministries, and we tithe our income and more. What can we do for Christ together?"

Finally, they decided, "Let's use our home for hospitality. We can invite uncommitted people over on Sunday nights after we take them to church with us." They went on to establish two Sundays a month for that purpose.

The idea is to plan together for a specific life of service for the Lord. People are drawn together by such common interests. We ask our husbands and wives to pray and develop together a life plan or goal. Most wives love to see their husbands take the lead here. Lawrence J. Crabb, Jr.'s, *Marriage Builder* is helpful reading, as is Robert E. Coleman's *Master Plan of Evangelism*.

Have a Spiritual Project

Part of the work of the advanced group is to embark the couple on spiritual projects. One couple wanted to work with people in need as their life plan. Marge got an assignment from the group leader.

She was introduced to a woman who was an alcoholic and in much trouble. No sooner did Marge begin to meet with her for prayer and Bible study than the woman was jailed for drunkenness. It was arranged for

180

Marge and another woman to visit her in the city jail. Neither woman had been inside a jail, and they were apprehensive at best. When they were admitted to the inner cell block and the iron doors clanged shut with a terrible thud, Marge really felt closed in. But with her partner, she approached the woman in her cell and began to witness and pray with her. Two more visits were made before the woman was released, but during those visits, Marge and her partner led the woman to know Jesus as Lord. The woman was baptized.

Marge will tell you today that she grew a lot through that experience. She had been exposed to a need and then allowed herself to be stretched so that her faith was strengthened. After that initiation, nothing seemed too hard for her faith to overcome. By becoming accountable with her husband to a group of other accountable believers, both Marge and her husband grew in the grace of God. In the process, they grew closer together.

Attitude on the Job

A person's attitude and performance on the job has to be a vital part of his accountability to the group. If he has an authority problem with his superior at work, there is magnificent instruction in Romans 13:7: "Render therefore to all their due: taxes to whom taxes are due, customs to whom customs, fear to whom fear, honor to whom honor." There are other verses in the Bible that speak about doing good work. But in our day, we need to stress honor to whom honor is due. Too many people today fail to understand that honoring the employer is a part of honoring the Lord, since all authority comes from God and is given to men.

When members of the group indicate problems on their jobs, the remedy must begin with their own attitudes. A first question should be, "How is your relationship with the person in charge?"

When Bud LaCore was in the tire business, he had an employee who was difficult to manage. The fellow simply would not take instructions. Finally, Bud led the man out to the street and turned him around so he could see the sign over the store. Bud said to the difficult employee, "What does that sign up there say?" The man answered, "It says, 'LaCore Tire Company'." With that, Bud answered, "I'm LaCore."

Helping someone learn who is in charge is a great benefit to him. All of us need to take instructions and accept correction if we are going to be productive. Would-be Christian leaders, who are seeking to be discipled, should be helped to see that resistance to authority on the job is actually an indication of their unwillingness to accept authority elsewhere. Followed to its logical conclusion, it would seem that those who struggle with the authority of others also struggle with the authority of the Lord Jesus Christ in their lives.

A good report at work is essential for a Christian leader. When a problem at work is posed before the accountability group, the members of the group will advise and help. The friendly pressure to improve, applied by group members to one another, is sometimes humorous—and supereffective.

Their Ministry in the Church

Some Christians have miserable attitudes about their churches, as though their spiritual lives apart from Sunday were separate from their involvement with God's people and the authority of their pastors. The accountability group can work as a small church to dispel those ideas and develop a strong commitment to the local church and its pastor. A Bible study on the nature and work of the church can be most helpful to the group.

There is a danger in accountability groups. If they are not under the umbrella of the local church, some members of the group can get superspiritual. They will fly by reality, aloof to the hard work that it takes to operate a church and reach a community for Christ. That is a danger! So the group members must all be accountable for their lives in the church, for prayer, witness, service, stewardship, worship, attitude, and total commitment.

Witness in the Community

Accountability, or lack of it, really shows in the way a Christian lives in his community. Each member, especially in the advanced group, must deal with those areas of personal life in which the person is weak. We have already touched on the attitude on the job, and we talked about how the earlier group pledged to be honest in their dealings in the community.

There are other areas, too. A Christian leader must learn to live within his means. He cannot be a compulsive shopper, and he must manage his affairs to stay out of debt, no matter how small his income. If he gets a bad credit rating, his name will be on the list of every merchant in town who gets that report. The group can help here. If financial counseling is needed, they can help arrange it.

Group members should become accountable for their business dealings in the community. The church once elected a man to the board of deacons who had a poor business reputation. In fact, when it was known around town that he had become a deacon, I received a barrage of phone calls from people who complained. A typical statement was, "Do you know what this man has been doing in this community? With him on your board, I will never darken the door of your church." What could be done? First of all, I have never taken kindly to threats from people who have never darkened the door of the church anyway. But, the problem remained. Because of his irresponsible and sometimes underhanded business dealings, the deacon should not have been elected. What could be done?

I met with the man and explained my concern about the complaints I had received. I attempted to help him see that he needed to apply Christian ethics to his business dealings. We met often for prayer and then he got involved in an accountability group. The result of his group involvement was immediate and lasting. He not only changed his style in the business world, the man became a genuine spiritual leader. He became what every nominating committee should look for in a deacon. It is true that leaders are made, not born.

Accountability groups are not for everybody because some church members are not ready to submit to God or the authority of His church. Selection of the group members should be carefully undertaken. Only those who honestly wish to improve their testimonies and the quality of their lives should be chosen. But the most important selection of all should be choosing the group leader.

Time - Management Survey
Weekly Schedule

	SUN	MON	TUES	WED	THURS	FRI	SAT
5:30 a.m.							
6:00							
6:30							
7:00							
7:30							
8:00							
8:30							
9:00							
9:30							
10:00							
10:30							
11:00							
11:30							
12:00 noon							
12:30							
1:00							
1:30							
2:00							
2:30							
3:00							
3:30							
4:00							
4:30							
5:00							
5:30							
6:00							
6:30							
7:00							
7:30							
8:00							
8:30							
9:00							
9:30							
10:00							
10:30							
11:00							
11:30							
12:00							
12:30							
1:00							

STEWARDSHIP OF TIME

Quiet Time _____
Study of the Word _____
Meditation _____
Christian Service _____
Rest _____

Recreation _____
Social Time _____
Athletics _____
Employment _____
Family Time _____

Miscellaneous _____
Television _____
Telephone _____
TOTAL TIME _____

The Reward Is Worth the Struggle

The best advice on problem solving I ever got came from a Christian leader who was about to retire from the ministry. I asked him how he had managed to keep his joy while persevering for the Lord over a long time.

His answer tells his story. "I always understood that God saved me for a purpose. When I found out what that purpose was—what my life's work was to be—I determined to stick to it. But I knew that Christ was with me. I determined to walk close to Him."

That was a tremendous answer! But he added a second thought that has gotten me through some troubled times. "I have always regarded the trouble of the day as just that—trouble for one day. I have made it a practice never to carry trouble with me overnight. And God has always made it His practice to work out the problems when I pray and start looking for His answers."

Here was a man of faith filled with the kind of spiritual optimism that allows for failures and temporary setbacks but always sees through to victory.

Have an Optimistic Point of View

Faith makes us optimists. It enables us to see possibilities for the expansion of God's kingdom that might be invisible to others whose vision is clouded by difficulties. Success or failure will depend upon the way we approach matters, especially when there are problems to be solved.

The story about two salesmen who had different views of the same situation illustrates the difference between the faithful optimist and the faithless pessimist. Two shoe salesmen went to a backward country to look for a possible market for their shoes. But at the place they visited, the people did not wear shoes. The first salesman returned home with a discouraging report. He said, "There is no market for shoes in the area we visited. No one wears shoes in that place." The second salesman said, "The market for shoes there is unlimited. No one is wearing shoes, but they all need them."

I would suggest that a spiritual leader in the Church of Jesus Christ has more cause for optimism than anyone else in all the world. He, above all people, should see through faithful eyes and look to what God can do in every situation. A man of faith will look through the surface problem to see the possibility of a big win for the Lord's side. But the motivated leader made optimistic by faith will need to be spiritually equipped to make the hard decisions required in problem solving.

Equip Yourself with Spiritual Armor

Let everyone who would lead in Christ's church take seriously those words of Scripture that begin "Finally,

187

my brethren, be strong in the Lord and in the power of His might" and that instruct us to "put on the whole armor of God" (Eph. 6:10–11). In verse 11, the reason for needing God's armor is made clear, "that you may be able to stand against the wiles of the devil."

The "wiles of the devil" speaks of his treachery. He can make a small problem seem like an insurmountable obstacle. When your trouble seems overwhelming, you might be looking at an illusion, a tempest in a teapot. It is common for a spiritual leader to spend a sleepless night wrestling with a superproblem that seems to threaten the foundations of the church only to find in the light of day that the problem was insignificant and manageable. My friend's advice on not carrying trouble with you overnight will be helpful.

However, sometimes troubles are as big as they seem. When that happens, read on, "For we do not wrestle against flesh and blood, but against principalities, against powers, against the rulers of the darkness of this age, against spiritual hosts of wickedness in the heavenly places" (Eph. 6:12). That is when you will need God's armor, when you are engulfed in spiritual warfare.

Victory over the unseen enemy in spiritual warfare does not come by merely developing human skills. The answer we seek is in Scripture. Verse 13 of Ephesians 6 continues the thought, "Therefore take up the whole armor of God, that you may be able to withstand in the evil day, and having done all, to stand." While the whole armor of God is required, I want to emphasize the need of faith that is so essential in times of stress and trouble. Verse 16 says, ". . . above all, taking the shield of faith with which you will be able to quench all the fiery darts of the wicked one."

In the thick of battle, it is the shield of faith that protects and empowers us to trust in God and not in ourselves. My biggest problems have come when I have failed to remember that I am not alone.

In facing difficulties, spiritual preparation is the first order of the day. Prayer, Bible reading, meditation, and the prayerful encouragement of others in the faith give the spiritual renewal needed to deal with the problems we face.

Problems Are Common to Us All

When you do face problems, do not be overwhelmed. Problems are common to us all. The manager of a Sears store once told me, "Managing the church is much like managing the store. Just when you have everything organized and going well, things begin to fall in on you."

It is important for a leader to recognize that problems are always going to occur as long as we are in the world. But the difference between a winner and a loser is the way they meet and handle problems. There will be times when, for the umbrella man, it seems as though the wheels have fallen off the entire program. But if he deals with problems wisely, he will contribute mightily to the strength and vitality of the body of Christ.

The reason that problems are common to us all has to do with human nature. Understanding human nature is a real part of wisdom, but you have to get that understanding without becoming discouraged.

When I was an assistant pastor and about to be left alone with responsibility for a flock for the first time, the pastor's parting words put the situation in focus for me. He said, "Remember, we are all sinners. Don't expect one hundred percent and you won't be disappointed." He was simply telling me not to be naive.

Here are some rules of life to take into account, especially when plans go wrong.

1. *Every believer is in process.* No one arrives at perfection in this life. Therefore, do not be surprised when others stumble.

2. *Imperfect people make mistakes.* Do not accept mediocrity as a norm, but do not be discouraged when mistakes are made.

3. *Spiritual vitality will ebb and flow in accordance with a person's motivation and spiritual intake.* Make sure there is plenty of spiritual food, but invest your best efforts in the motivated ones. The others can come along when they are ready.

4. *Sinners can change.* Do not tag people as losers because they have failed previously. Allow the grace of God to work in them as it has worked in you.

5. *Keep the right perspective on your own life.* It is good to remember that other people see in you what you do not see. That thought will help to keep you humble. Your periodic failures will do the trick if all else fails.

Watch Out for Self-pity

I once asked a woman, who worked long hours serving in the church, "What is your biggest problem?"

Without a blink of an eye, she answered, "Self-pity."

Her reply surprised me because she seemed to be always smiling and highly motivated. And she never complained! When I asked her to explain she answered, "I know I have a tendency to look at others who are doing less, and wonder why I have to do it all. When I get into that pattern, self-pity comes in on me and penetrates right to my bones like a cold morning fog."

Then she went on to explain her way to victory. "I have to begin every day thanking God and praising Him for health and physical vitality. Then I thank Him for my church as my place to serve the Lord and grow spiritually. I praise God for my pastor. Along the way I read the Scripture. And then I sing a chorus—just between God and me. And then, just before I begin to do my work, I remind myself that what I do I do for the Lord."

Self-pity is debilitating! It happens when the human spirit turns in upon itself. When two self-pitiers get together the effect seems more than doubled. When this happens, the Holy Spirit appears to be ruled out altogether, as far as joy and motivation are concerned.

Elijah did not need someone to commiserate with him. When the prophet ran from his enemies, he was more than afraid. I think he felt sorry for himself. When God caught up with Elijah and asked him what he was doing in the cave, his answer gives that insight. "I have been very zealous for the LORD God of hosts; for the children of Israel have forsaken Your covenant, torn down Your altars, and killed Your prophets with the sword. I alone am left; and they seek to take my life" (1 Kings 19:10).

The heavy emphasis on "I" and "my" tells the story. In his confrontation with the prophets of Baal, though, the subject of Elijah's conversation had been God. Later, when he looked at the awesome conflict on Mount Carmel, he got to thinking about himself and became concerned for his own well-being. His fear and self-pity seem to have been interlocked.

It seems that the woman who had learned how to deal with her tendency toward self-pity had the answer to Elijah's problem also.

Another way to put her answer to self-pity is keep your eyes and your thoughts on God. Be thankful for the opportunity to serve Him. Make Him the centerpiece of your conversation. Let the Holy Spirit dominate your human spirit. Get the right mind-set each day. Here is a word from God that has helped me mightily in this regard. "Set your mind on things above, not on things on the earth. For you died, and your life is hidden with Christ in God" (Col. 3:2–3).

On the battlefield, soldiers who expect to die and even feel as though they are already dead tend to live longer. In fact, they will be more likely to come home than those who are more tentative and less apt to throw themselves wholeheartedly into battle.

We have actually already died in Christ. Now we can be free to live with abandon.

That is what Paul meant when he said, "I have been crucified with Christ; it is no longer I who live, but Christ lives in me; and the life which I now live in the flesh I live by faith in the Son of God, who loved me and gave Himself for me" (Gal. 2:20).

Here are some problems I have faced that have required the kind of attitudes and spiritual preparation that have been described thus far.

When Staff Cutbacks Are Necessary

Adding staff members to the church is usually a joyful occasion. However, financial pressures can make cutting back on staff positions difficult. This means releasing someone from his job, a decision of the toughest kind. How can such a hard decision be implemented?

During the recession in the early 1980s we had to shorten our staff because the church was overextended financially. In January, we discussed the problem openly in the staff meeting and began to pray, asking God to show who among us should move out. By April, the time had come to make the change. After much prayer, we began to understand who would move. One of the men received a call from another church during our weeks of prayer.

When I talked to him about the move he said, "My wife and I have prayed and gotten the answer!" There was a witness of the Spirit there; through prayer, I had come to believe that he should be the one to move. The young couple, willing to follow God's call, had already received their answer.

It is always best to approach a problem openly and honestly. When we pray, God answers. He moves His servants in His own way.

When a Staff Member Does Not Work Out

Another difficult decision will have to be made when someone on staff is over his head and unable to do his work. After many attempts have been made to help him, something must be done to remedy the situation.

Rather than fire the person, as is the way of the world, it is better if another job can be found that is not too demanding for him. If possible, further training should be arranged so that he can qualify for a better job.

If help is given to move the unqualified worker to ground he can handle, both he and the church are helped. The important thing is to be up front and to have his interest at heart.

But in recommending someone to another pastor or employer, in order to move him on, care must always be taken to be honest with the recommendation. If you cannot recommend him, do not.

When a Worker's Interest Changes

Many young men begin their ministries as youth pastors but later feel that God wants them to preach. This is a common occurrence in the church. How can the transition be made? Start by being open and honest about the needed change. Have the worker's interest at heart, as well as the ongoing work of the ministry.

Trouble can come if the youth minister tries to satisfy his call to preach in the youth groups. When this happens, there are two problems. The young people are hearing more preaching than they can handle. And if he is not properly directed, the youth pastor might find himself competing with his pastor. This has happened more than once. However, instead of viewing a change of focus in ministry as a problem, it is better to regard it as God's way of developing His servants.

I have talked to numbers of such young men who feel they should follow the call to preach. If more training is needed, I encourage them to get it. And if their seminary work is concluded and they are ready to go out, I want to help them secure locations for preaching.

The key is to recognize what is happening and be as helpful as possible with the man's transition to a new ministry. Failure in leadership here will stifle the growth of the church and the youth pastor.

When a Staff Member Is Called Away

Sometimes when a fellow worker is called away to another church, it is difficult to accept the move as the Lord's will; here is a person who is important to the work, with valuable relationships developed among God's people who love him, and he is leaving. You know that the church will miss his productivity. But as God's will is recognized, steps must be taken to help the man move and to help the people of the church accept it as God's call.

As soon as a decision is reached and the time of departure is established, an announcement should be made. It is good if the one leaving can make the announcement, so there will be no question about why he is leaving. This helps protect the church against rumors that the man was unfairly dealt with or run off.

In one church where the departure of a staff member was not handled properly, the pastor was later falsely accused of getting rid of the man. Later, he spent countless hours running down rumors and gossip that put the relationship of the pastor and the former associate pastor in a bad light.

Fortunately, the relationship of the two men had been good and had remained so. The false accusation finally was cleared up. But it would have been easier if the proper announcements had been made, together with adequate thanks and a glorious send-off.

Let partings be joyful and filled with appreciation for the years the person has been allowed by God to spend in the work. Umbrella men who walk with God will consider the departure of a staff member as a mission for service, according to the will of God. So it was in the early church when Paul and Barnabas were sent to the Gentiles. "As they ministered to the LORD and fasted, the Holy Spirit said, 'Now separate to Me Barnabas and Saul for the work to which I have called them.' Then, having fasted and prayed, and laid hands on them, they sent them away" (Acts 13:2–3).

When Deacons Don't "Deac"

Members of official boards often do not function as they should. Often people are chosen for leadership responsibilities who are spiritually immature and unqualified for the work of ministry. When this happens, instead of being frustrated and filled with self-pity, develop a plan and set it in motion.

The plan should have two parts. "Plan A" is to help develop the spiritual life of the nonfunctioning or malfunctioning board member and, in the process, train him to function in a leadership role.

I once set out to help a deacon who was elected to the board for all the wrong reasons. He was chosen at random and nominated in an open meeting. The man was personable and friendly, but he had absolutely no training in discipleship. His grasp of the Bible was nil, and he had no real idea of how the church operated.

In that church the deacons made all of the policy decisions. So his responsibility was great. He failed miserably. At every turn he was afraid to make decisions and found it easy to oppose them. Soon he began to miss meetings. His attitude turned negative—then completely sour. I could not remove him. What could be done? Improvement was the only answer.

I began to meet with him on Thursdays for lunch. We

began to pray together and study portions of the Bible. I introduced him to commentaries and Bible helps. Along the way we talked about stewardship and commitment to the ministry of the church. In the process we became friends and partners in the ministry.

Through that experience and many others like it, I am convinced that ordinary people, even nonfunctioning people, can become great servants of God if they are properly led and discipled.

Still, there is a "Plan B." If the discipleship effort meets with no response, the plan is to endure with patience. Pray, make do with what you have to work with, and set up proper qualifications and procedures to ensure that the same mistake is not made again. On such occasions I have prayed, "Lord, help me to be patient. But Lord, let's find another member for the board next time."

Resolve here not to settle for the debilitating, Spirit-quenching leadership selection of the past. Find ways to upgrade the system! I have learned to disciple people and prepare them before they are nominated. I have also learned that church leaders are developed, not discovered.

Begin with a Problem, End with a Victory

Until we face our problems, we cannot win victories God has planned for us. Here is an account of a pastor who had plenty of troubles, but his story has a happy ending, which is still in progress at this writing.

For sixteen years the pastor labored to build up a small church. He worked long hours each day, toiling with his hands to build the church facility. In the evenings, he changed clothes and went out to visit prospects for the church and to minister to those already in his flock.

Then late at night and early in the morning, the pastor prayed to God for His blessing upon the work. He was faithful to preach with all his heart every Sunday, and His sermons were biblical. But they lacked power. No matter how hard he worked, the church did not grow.

With fatigue came discouragement. After years of hard work and sacrifice, God's man was finished in the ministry. He knew he could not go on at the pace he had kept in the past. He also knew that the return on his labor had been minimal. One hundred sixty members would make a good beginning, but that small number should not mark the total effort of a man's life ministry. He knew that each member of his flock was important. But he felt that he could have multiplied it far more.

Then, when he was at his lowest ebb, the pastor learned about some of the quiet qualities of leadership discussed in this book. He determined to set some priorities, and for the first time in his sixteen years he saw the possibility of getting someone to help him. He decided on the priorities of staff, program, and facilities.

First he had to get some rest. For the first time in several years, the pastor took a vacation. It was only for two weeks, and for the first week he could not get away. His mind kept wandering back to the problems he had left behind. But the second week he was able to let go and enjoy himself with his wife and family.

Immediately upon his return, he looked for an associate pastor to help with Christian education. A man was called, but the arrangement did not work out. In his desperation to get help, the pastor had not been careful enough in selecting his first staff member. Now the original problem was exacerbated. What could be done?

Wisely, the two men sat down together and discussed the reality of the situation. They had tried to make it work over a period of two years, but their philosophies of ministry were different. They were not pulling together. The pastor was honest and open with the associate. He admitted his mistake in a hurried call, and he offered to help the other minister relocate. They prayed together until the man could find another place to serve and then parted as friends.

Undaunted, the pastor looked for another associate but this time more carefully. When none could be found, he discovered that God had raised up such a man within the congregation.

The man was a college graduate but had no formal seminary training. However, it was determined that the new associate could learn as he went along, using conferences and short training courses when available. The new man's biggest asset was that he shared the pastor's philosophy, and his work record in the church was excellent. He was a student of the Bible and equipped already for the ministry before him in that regard. Best of all, he and the pastor knew each other well. They were already friends. They were compatible.

Having new priorities, the pastor stopped working on buildings and began to spend more time in his study. Power began to come to his preaching, and the church began to grow. Within a year the congregation grew to over three hundred. With the church crowded, a decision to build a new sanctuary was discussed.

Then the pastor remembered the priorities—staff, program, facilities. He convinced the people to wait on the new building and add to the pastoral staff instead. In that way they could also train the laity better. They would build programs around their new staff and thus add more people. Outreach was most important to the church. The people caught the pastor's vision.

The third man, an evangelism pastor, was added. He led the church in a lay witness program that prompted the members to share their faith in Christ. The results were startling. New Christians were added to the church each week in such numbers that the church buildings could not hold them all.

With numerical growth came the need to revise the church's decision-making apparatus. They had operated by the town hall method, airing every detail of church business before the entire congregation. But because the people were involved in witnessing and discipling ministries, they were ready to move to a more representative government. With surprising unanimity, the church shifted to a one-board system of government. They chose the diaconate model. The streamlined system left the responsibility for most decisions in the hands of a small elected group, while the majority of the people were free for ministry.

With the crowds came the need to have a second service each Sunday morning. Teen-agers were everywhere, it seemed. And it was apparent that a youth pastor was needed. The search for an experienced youth man took time, but the pastor located a highly effective man in another city. This time, care was taken to make sure the new man would be able to work with the pastor and the associate pastors.

To everyone's delight, the youth pastor was like a pied piper. He drew young people into the church and brought them to Christ. He was the kind of leader who could get a crowd of young people together, and he knew how to disciple them when he did.

The congregation was getting large and a new sanctuary and some education buildings were badly needed. But what was good about waiting for the new sanctuary was that the leadership then knew to build big enough to hold the crowds.

The story is still unfolding, but it is safe to say that through the perseverance of an enlightened pastor and a productive staff victories will continue. A struggling pastor has become an umbrella man.

In reflecting on his struggles to build up the church of God, the pastor said, "Back there when I was exhausted and ready to give it all up, the struggle didn't seem worth continuing. But now that I have found my way, let me tell you—*the reward is worth the struggle*." "To him who overcomes I will grant to sit with Me on My throne, as I also overcame and sat down with My Father on His throne" (Rev. 3:21).

Epilogue: Two Little Words

There are two little words that should be heard more often throughout the Church of Jesus Christ today. These two little words are "thank you."

Those who serve the Lord should learn the importance of thankfulness toward God and toward one another. How beautiful it is when God's people are thankful to Him and show their gratitude in praise and thanksgiving! How encouraging it is to those who labor on behalf of others to know their work is appreciated!

In this book I have spoken much of leadership and how leaders are to provide for others. Here, then, is a major contribution: let all who would develop their leadership skills give a high priority to the expressing of thanks.

Saying "thank you" to others is essential to the leader who will keep himself on track by reminding himself that he does not do what he does alone. God has provided the leader with fellow workers who, while serving their Lord, are serving with him.

A sincere word of thanks will help your coworker to know that he or she is accepted and appreciated. The need to know that others approve and are appreciative is important to everyone. How sad it is, then, when God's people who should be kind and considerate neglect so basic a need as this.

It has been said that gratefulness is the mark of a great man. Expressing gratitude, then, is not demeaning. On the contrary, it reveals the sensitivity and thoughtfulness that accompany spiritual maturity.

I have tried to be careful always to thank the congregation for their faithful ministry in the church and in the community. So often we preachers tell God's people what is wrong with them. We need to tell them what is right and thank them for it. In this we have the example of the apostle Paul, who wrote to the Philippians, "I thank my God upon every remembrance of you, always in every prayer of mine making request for you all with joy, for your fellowship in the gospel from the first day until now" (Phil. 1:3–5).

In the same way, Christian brethren should reflect on the faithful service of men and women of God. This is especially so because evangelists, pastors, and teachers are given by God as gifts to His church.

Students for the ministry should be deeply grateful to those who quite literally have put their lives into them. True, the teacher gets great satisfaction from the success of a former pupil. But the pupil should remember to thank the teacher who helped equip him for the ministry he enjoys. Such thanksgiving acknowledges the marvelous working of the body of Christ.

Most of all, thanksgiving should be offered to God! The injunction in 1 Thessalonians 5:16–18 is well-known: "Rejoice always, pray without ceasing, in everything give thanks; for this is the will of God in Christ Jesus for you."

As a leader in Christ's church, I can tell you that becoming and remaining thankful to God for the life I live and the people I serve is the foundation for the good that comes my way. In human terms, giving thanks to God is rewarding *Him* for the struggle! My thanksgiving to God pleases Him. It keeps open channels of blessing for me and for the church where I serve. Furthermore, that spirit of thanksgiving is recognizable to the people of the church. And it is catching. As a personal blessing, thanksgiving keeps me joyful. It causes me to study to be appreciative—to look on the bright side. When the umbrella man is thankful, the people he serves will be thankful as well.

For more reason than hoping for what thanksgiving does for us, we must look to God and offer our continuing thanksgiving to Him. For those of us who express the quiet qualities of leadership that are gifts from God, let Paul's words of thanksgiving be our prayer.

And I thank Christ Jesus our Lord who has enabled me, because He counted me faithful, putting me into the ministry (1 Tim. 1:12).